31 Days to
BRAVE

31 Days to BRAVE

LETTING GO OF FEAR AND TRAUMA
ONE STEP AT A TIME

KATHY SMALLEY

Carpenter's Son Publishing

Published by Carpenter's Son Publishing, Franklin, Tennessee

Cover and Interior Design by Suzanne Lawing

Printed in the United States of America

978-1-954437-84-5

Dedication

To the four brave heroes in my life—Brett, Sarah Beth, Garrett, and Abby Kate! Thank you for trusting me, for your constant patience and love, and for making this life so beautiful! You four have stood in the fire, stood with each other, and chosen to rise above with grace and greatness. Being your mom will forever be my greatest joy and most epic accomplishment!

We'd love to hear from you!

Kathy Smalley is available for book signings and speaking engagements. We look forward to connecting with you! You may email us at kathy@kathysmalley.com, or message Kathy on her website at www.kathysmalley.com.

Social Media:

@kathyroseberrysmalley

@kathydsmalley

Contents

Be strong and of good courage

Deuteronomy 3:16

INTRODUCTION

*T*hank you for being brave enough to pick up this book! You probably are searching for something more and you desire the courage and practical steps to move forward in your life. Pain is pain, and your pain may be monumental and debilitating or at the least, frustrating and exhausting. The good news I'm here to share with you is God really cares. He is reaching for your hand and He longs to lead you into all He has for you! My prayer is that *31 Days to Brave* will push you through the indecision and inaction that keeps many from the bravery and victory God has for us. Each step in this book will build you up and begin to reframe your world as you grow in courage and ownership of all that is already inside of you.

31 Days to Brave comes from my journey to becoming brave. Becoming (and being) brave is a forever faith journey; yet I believe as we courageously take brave steps, God always meets us in such a marvelous way! I have walked through the death of a loved one, a devastating divorce, and the darkness of living with an addict. As a licensed therapist, I have witnessed the effects of trauma in the lives of countless others as well as my own. I have seen and experienced the overwhelming grace of God and I know that there is always a way *through* the pain, and that there is always hope in Christ. In Isaiah 61:3, God promises to give us a crown of beauty for ashes. One of the "crowns of beauty" that came from the ashes of my trauma is that I "found my BRAVE!"

I pray that through *31 Days to Brave*, you will find the empowerment and peace that comes from bravely choosing to step forward with Christ instead of succumbing to depression, anxiety and hopelessness. With simple and consistent steps, you can build and control your own future!

Obviously, we cannot always control things that happen to us, but with Christ's help, we can take back the power and responsibility of our future.

I think there is a big misconception that one day we will just wake up and be brave! Or if we just "believe" enough, then we will find our courage. We don't just get the bravery to believe, we must act our way out by taking steps (even baby ones) to build belief in ourselves. Depression is not just going to simply break, nor is anxiety going to just go away. The reality is that we must come into partnership with God and take practical steps to build bravery. He will meet us right where we are, and He has given us the power of the Holy Spirit to help us!

God promises in John 11:40 that we will see His glory (God in all His goodness and power), if we will just believe. But how do we believe when our hearts and lives have been shipwrecked by trauma or difficulty, leaving us in utter despair, pain or even numbness? How do we get from the promise to the fulfillment? Jeremiah 29:11 says, *"For I know the plans I have for you, plans of good and not of evil, plans to give you a hope and a future."* I love that verse, but I remember during some of the darkest nights of my soul not having the capacity to believe it. Maybe you feel that way right now. Maybe you don't see any hope at all. Maybe you feel stuck, fearful or frustrated. *31 Days to Brave* is for anyone (like me) who found themselves in the depths of trauma, unable to neither get out of the past nor able to see a future. I was desperate for a shred of direction and hope. This little book is my gratitude to God for taking me by the hand and leading me out of the darkness and into the light. This book is me reaching for your hand and gently leading you to know practically where to start. It won't always be easy, but I know that if you will trust the process, you too will find that you can take courage!

I

THIS CAN'T BE TRUE

I was sitting on the sofa, dozing off when my husband's phone buzzed. It shook me out of sleep, my eyes looking around to see where the buzz had come from. I had never really checked his phone because I really didn't think about things like that. But that night I nonchalantly picked it up and it was an email from a woman I didn't recognize.

"Had so much fun! (Heart emoji) Can't wait to see you again!"

I sat up straighter and clicked on it and blinked my eyes to focus on the words again. Surely this is not what I think it is!? Surely not. I continued to read to my horror.

My heart began to beat faster as the words and its meaning dawned on me. My husband came into the room just then and flipped on the light.

"Is this what I think it is?" I blurted out and couldn't stop myself, "Are you having an affair?"

I felt the blood rush from my face even as I said that. I felt dizzy. I felt sick. A thousand emotions flooded me at one time. I tried to breathe as I stared at my husband across the room.

My heart silently begged for him to give me the logical explanation and stop the shock that was quickly taking over. Soon he would come over, put his arms around me and we would talk this through and all would be well.

But that didn't happen.

His eyes grew wide with defensive rage and out of his mouth came the poison that would surely turn my life upside down. Obviously, it was true. He'd been caught in his lies and left screaming, "You might as well know everything now".

To be honest, the rest of that night is a blur, as well as the days and even weeks following. The unraveling and revealing of betrayal is an unexplainable crushing. If you've experienced betrayal, you know exactly what I'm talking about. It's like your mind cannot comprehend the truth. You've been living in a world that you know, and suddenly what you thought of the world isn't real anymore. Everything is flipped upside down. It is the same with all different kinds of grief or trauma. Maybe you have lost someone you loved, maybe you received a diagnosis that was a heavy blow. That is what trauma does. Trauma takes your true identity and flips it upside down, seemingly stripping you of everything you have previously believed to be true along with the future you thought was secure.

Sometimes, spouses spend months feeling crazy and digging for the revelation, other times it hits them like a runaway train like it did me. Either way, we are ultimately left with a choice. And it's not easy by any definition. Many times, we would rather just stick our head in the sand like an ostrich and hope it goes away. We don't want to confront. We don't want our reality to be rocked. We don't want to be there in that situation! I can't count how many times I said those very words, "I just don't want to be here" (and I wasn't referencing a location!) I literally didn't want to be in the space of having to face reality! I remember when my brother was killed suddenly in an accident, there were moments I would be going along about my day, and then once again the reality would come slamming in and I would have to face it again, "Kathy, your brother died." It was so surreal and confusing. Different people react in different ways to a traumatic event, but every person who goes through a trauma ultimately comes to a point where they must face the hard reality.

How do we survive in those unexplainable agonizing events? I think it's by the grace of God that our brains often go into shock. It is a form of self-preservation, but after the shock always comes the reality. So, how do we "face reality"? How do we force ourselves to accept the reality that things we believed were actually lies, or life as we knew it no longer exists? It's a process. It's a very hard process and it takes great courage to walk through the heartaches and pain and SEE and receive the truth!

I'm sharing this with you because we can and will overcome! God won't leave you in the trauma without a way to live again. He will not leave you to suffer without hope and without healing! But it starts with realizing that if you've experienced something drastic or traumatic, your world has been flipped upside down and your heart turned inside out. As you stay with me for this 31 Days to Brave journey, I believe and know that God will begin to turn you right side up again. I feel for you. I ache for you. You are not alone, though I know it may truly feel like it. So, if all you can do right now is nod your head and let the tears roll, it's okay. You are not going to feel this way forever. All I'm asking is that you let God take you by the hand and gently comfort and lead you, step by step. As reality smacks you in the face, just remember those words, "You are NOT going to feel this way forever!" There is hope and your life is not over. Hold on and fall into His arms as He begins to set you on your feet again.

―――――――― *Rise To Brave!* ――――――――

Today, I want you to simply read this prayer over yourself. It takes great courage in pain to even read a page or two. I understand that. Turn on a worship song. If you don't know one, I'm going to suggest Cece Winans' song, "Goodness of God." Take heart, beautiful soul…you are making a brave step right now. I'm praying for YOU.

God, I don't feel like praying right now, but here I am. I feel like I've been hit by a huge truck and so much of the time I feel like I can't breathe. So Holy Spirit, help me to even read this out loud.

God, your Word says that You are good, and Your loving kindness is everlasting and Your faithfulness is to all generations (Psalm 100:6). You are FOR me, (Your name) so who can be against me? (Romans 8:31). Jeremiah 29:11 says that You have a plan for me, (Your name), and that it is good and not evil and it's a plan with a FUTURE and a HOPE. God, I want to believe these promises of Yours, and yet it's hard right now. You promise that all things are possible if I believe (Mark 11:23), so Lord please help my unbelief (Mark 9:24). Thank You Lord that You go before me, will be with me and will never leave me nor forsake me (Deuteronomy 31:8). I know that not one of Your promises is empty of power and that nothing is impossible with

God. (Luke 1:37). So, I'm asking right now for your courage. In Jesus name, Amen.

If you are not dealing with trauma or facing something hard right now, think of someone you know that is. Take the time to pray this over them and maybe send them this prayer right now.

For with God nothing shall be impossible.

Luke 1:37

2

THE TABLE

I walked out into my backyard as the sun was rising on a beautiful spring day. It was something that I usually did to feel peace and talk to the Lord. It had been months and months since I had any landscape done on our once beautiful yard. Addiction had emptied bank accounts and I couldn't afford the landscape upkeep and it made me sad to see all the overgrown bushes, dead flowers and the unkempt yard. I looked over on the patio where the 12-foot family table sat. A gentle smile crossed my face as I remembered all six of us sitting around that table, laughing and eating. We had made some incredible memories there. Yet the table, like the rest of the formerly serene backyard, was now broken, cracked and disheveled from the lack of attention and wear from the storms. I sighed as I thought how apropos that was. It was such a picture of my life at that moment—beaten down and stripped of its luster. The table looked like I felt.

The more I stared at it, the madder I got. Something rose inside me and the anger about my current circumstances and what the enemy had stolen moved me into action. I thought to myself, "No, it won't ever be the same, it will be different. But, dang it, IT WILL BE BETTER." I was resolved.

I found a tape measure and measured the width and length. I got into my son's mustang and headed to Home Depot without a clue on how to replace a tabletop, but come hell or high water, I was going to do it! I knew I needed a drill. All 5' 2" of me was marching through Home Depot, determined to bravely rebuild that table. I remember asking a worker what drill I needed. Somehow, I had heard of the Dewalt brand and asked about it. The guy showed me a few less expensive drills that were in my budget, but it was like I was going for the gold and wanted the best shoes! So, I bought the best drill. Then I picked out wood for the top. I picked out wood that was thicker and prettier than the original tabletop and had the store cut it the right length. I purchased a sander and staining supplies and headed to the car. The Home Depot worker looked alarmed when I pulled up in the Mustang and he expressed how it wouldn't fit. He obviously did not understand my determination. I reassured him I wasn't driving far and laid the seats down and told him to let it hang out the back… I was on a mission!

I began my big brave task with a fervency. I was going to rebuild the entire table, but what I didn't know was what God was going to do *inside* of me. The process became such a huge healing experience! I could sense the gentleness of the Holy Spirit as He related it all to the rebuilding of my own life through Christ. The entire endeavor was the best therapy I could have done for myself. I felt the hope of God as I saw the tabletop being restored.

The legs of the table were distressed wood to begin with and now they served as a reminder that the foundation of my life would still be the same and the Lord was rebuilding, refurbishing, and restoring me to a beautiful and better life. All the good foundation that had been laid in my journey (just like the original table legs) would not be wasted but serve as a part of the beauty God would bring from the ashes of my life. The stripping of the old table (God stripping away the old narratives and lies), the calluses from working so hard with my hands (God healing the tearing of my soul), the smoothing of the top (God smoothing the rough places in my life) and even nicking my hand (sometimes it's painful in the process) were all great lessons of how God uses the difficult things we walk through to refine us to a restored place of glory.

The definition of the word restored exactly described what happened to my table,

RESTORED (def): Better than the original.

God was lovingly working in my life, building me back stronger and better. When I finished, my table was like a brand new and improved table—thicker, stronger, 10x prettier and super sturdy on its repainted, original, foundational legs.

Today, I can tell you that embracing your journey isn't always easy and it takes great courage; but it is so worth it! I could not have imagined at that time what beautiful things God had in store for me! He is so incredibly faithful! Bravery is built one step at a time and restoring and rebuilding my family table took lots of brave steps to just go for it! But, oh the joy of the finished product! I know God longs to do His work of rebuilding within us. All we must do is partner with Him and let His Spirit gently lead us each step of the way. He is the God of restoration, and He will restore you.

———————— *Rise To Brave!* ————————

Maybe today, you feel like I did. Maybe you feel broken and beaten down and need to recreate some things that will give you more clarity. To create more space in your life for abundance, renewed relationships, and new opportunities, you must declutter and complete things that can be a mental burden. What is a task or something in your life right now that needs redone, delegated, or completed? Maybe you have a closet that needs to be cleaned out, a room that needs repainting, a project that has been looming and the demands of life have kept you continuing to put it off. Today is your day to move towards a renewed future, refreshed mind, and rekindled passions! Make a list of things you need to tackle and choose two or three and start completing them. Maybe there is a big project that seems daunting or may even be out of your expertise, like my table. Ask God what specific things will build the most confidence and clarity once completed; things that He can also use to reveal more of Himself to you through the process. I promise you, no matter how small or big it is, God will speak to you through it as you seek Him and your spirit and mind will be wide open to the new possibilities you are making room for!

Write down one major thing in the space below you can commit to complete off your list before the end of this 31-day journey!

_____

_____

_____

*And I am sure of this,
that He who began a good
work in you will bring it to
completion until the day of
Christ Jesus.*

Philippians 1:6

3

PING PONG BALLS

So, life has thrown you a huge curveball, and an unexpected one at that! Most of us have heard about the stages of grief (Denial, Anger, Bargaining, Depression, Acceptance). Not everyone goes through all of them as described, because no one grieves the same way. I think one of the hardest things that I grieved initially was the "death" of what I thought my life would look like. Thoughts like "We were going to be the cutest grandparents together" or "What about my kids' wedding days?" "We were supposed to celebrate that together!" Or even "Why did that couple make it; we were happier than they were?" The "my life should be this or that" thoughts were brutal. I came to a point where I literally dealt with the "should haves' ", just so that I could move forward. I think fighting the pervading thoughts in our pain is one of the fiercest battles, but there is hope in taking it one step at a time.

I have a friend who went through a tragic loss of a child. I remember her saying to me some months after her loss, "It is what it is". That was hard for me to hear, but to her, it was her way of accepting the situation. There is some growth in being able to recognize that things are going to be different in the tangible realm; but I also want to share an illustration that a therapist friend of mine shared with me that made so much sense and kept me moving forward.

Painful emotions can be like sitting in a hot-tub and someone is dumping in 100 ping-pong balls all around you, then asking you to keep all 100 ping-pong balls under the water at the same time! If you've ever seen a ping-pong ball in a pool or tub of water, you know they are completely buoyant. They are lighter than the water, so they are almost impossible to sink and submerge— especially 100 at the same time! There is no way one person could hold all 100 ping-pong balls under the water at the same time—it is virtually impossible. Now, imagine those balls as representations of your trauma, thoughts or emotions, and picture yourself trying to just keep them 'under the water' to get rid of them! The only way to handle the ping-pong balls is to take one out at a time and set it out of the hot tub.

That illustration absolutely resonated with me. I remember the overwhelming variety of different emotions and thoughts that would hit me at random times and places. The more I tried to control ("push them under the water"), the more they popped up at inopportune times, unexpected ways and inappropriate places! As we learn to face the reality of our pain, choosing to address one aspect at a time (take one ping-pong ball out at a time) is one of the bravest and most courageous things we can do. When the thoughts and feelings are overwhelming or paralyzing, go back to baby steps. Take one thought, (picture it as one of the ping-pong balls with you in the hot tub), look at it, process it, and allow yourself to feel all the emotions. Then give it to God and set it aside.

What is one aspect of your pain or trauma that you need to let yourself pick up and set outside? What is one thing that you can face the reality of today? It may be as simple as "I'll have to shop alone." Whatever it is, big or small, pick it up and face the truth. Write it below and ask God to give you the strength to pick up one "ping pong ball" that you have been trying to "hold down under the water" and see it for what it is. God will give you the strength you need to face every reality.

The Lord is near to all who call on Him, to all who call on Him in truth.

Psalm 145:18 NASB

4

TAKE 100% RESPONSIBILITY FOR YOUR LIFE

My head was heavy, so heavy that it seemed like my neck couldn't carry it and generally, I felt like I had been hit by a truck. I had found solace in sleep which is often something that trauma and grief steals away. I would wake up each morning, have a moment of peace and then reality would slam me hard in the face.

"It wasn't a dream. This is my life."

I rolled over and put my feet on the ground in the same way I had for the last few weeks. I looked down at the dark, hand scraped wood floors beneath my feet and caught a glimpse of my running shoes in my peripheral vision lying alongside the wall of my bedroom. That still small voice came rushing in, "Get up and go run".

Everything within me wanted to crawl back in bed and envelop myself in the softness and safety of the blanket. It had been weeks of tears and fear from discovering facts that had been hidden and I was completely exhausted. As I glanced over at my running shoes one more time, I knew this was a pivotal moment that I needed to grab. I argued with myself on this decision and suddenly, strength came from my soul and I knew that I had to make a choice. I had to do something different, or I would stay trapped in grief. Most of us have been conditioned to blame someone or something for the things that go wrong in our life. So, bear in mind that when things happen that are completely out of our control, choosing to focus on the overwhelming present circumstances or the good that was lost will not move you forward into the life you desire.

Enough was enough.

The only person who could keep me from having the future I desired (for me and my children) was myself. It was time to take 100% responsibility for my life. It was up to me to decide to heal from the pain of my past and it was up to me to do my part to create a new future.

I got up, changed my clothes, walked immediately over to my running shoes, and laced them up. I was making a new decision and nothing that had been 'done' to me would be an excuse any longer. As a side note, I'll share a little trivia about me. I shave my legs every day. Every single day. I do it before I go workout in the morning because I don't like the feeling of wearing yoga pants when my legs aren't freshly shaved. Weird, I know. I own it.

I'm telling you that, so you know when I say I didn't shave my legs that morning before I put my running shoes on that there was a fire inside of me that had to move, to go, to change. I was compelled by the voice of the Holy Spirit. It was such a monumental crossroad. No past habit, no pain, shame, or blame was going to keep me walking in defeat or victimization. I was making a choice. I would no longer settle or live my life with excuses or allow the enemy to block me from running after what God had in store for me. I resolved that I was in charge of my future by the choices I made starting *that* day. I stopped blaming, making excuses and putting off what I knew was my responsibility. No matter what my past situation was, I was in charge of my healing and my future. For the first time in weeks, I felt an intense level of excitement and urgency. I had to start. Immediately.

I grabbed my air pods, headed out the door, and took off running. Nothing was going to keep me from the life I wanted and what I knew God had promised. I was going to *run* in search of everything He had for me.

And so, my journey began with small decisions and specific actions that led me day by day to a brand-new life. A life free from excuses or disappointment in myself. Just that one decision, not to hesitate, but to change my thinking and go running that day began the beginning of many consistent daily decisions that moved me from feeling like a victim to the liberating realization that I no longer had to live that narrative or give control over to what someone else said or did. When you take full responsibility for your life, you gain your power back over what is possible. God promises us a life abundant. I was the only one in control of my future of letting go and letting God rewrite the story of my life.

The hardest part of all this was accepting the knowledge that I could blame only myself for my future. That's a hard truth and one that we often avoid. **I decided to face my past and use it only as a point of reference and not a residence.** If you want to create the life of your dreams, then you must take full responsibility for your life too. That means giving up all excuses, all victim mentality, all blame, all the reasons why you can't and all the reasons why you haven't so far, as well as all excuses about your current circumstances. Remember....

You are the one who said yes to the project.

You are the one who stayed in the job.

You are the one who dated the guy.

You are the one who abandoned your dream.

You are the one who ate the donut.

You are the one who allowed them back into your life.

You are the one who said yes to the dog.

It took radical courage and resolve to *own my* part. The process, although simple, is not easy. It begins by deciding and taking just one step of action at a time.

List 2 situations in your life you are viewing as someone else's fault or something that was "done" to you that continues to affect you? How are you benefitting from this viewpoint? What price are you paying continuing this viewpoint?

_____

_____

_____

_____

_____

_____

_____

Now viewing your part in these situations, from a place of responsibility, what choices do you have for each situation?

Pick one thing you need to start taking responsibility for today. No beginning is too small.

Maybe it's a morning routine, maybe it's your emotional well-being, maybe it's forgiving someone, or maybe it's eating right. You probably know what it is. Ask God, listen and just start. Don't despise small beginnings.

Today I take responsibility for my myself and my future. I choose to view

_____

(situation) from a place of responsibility by

_____

(action steps).

And even if it is true that I have erred, my error remains with myself.

Job 19:4

5

FALSE NARRATIVES

*A*s you begin to face the truth in your situation a little at a time, you may realize that there were many lies that became YOUR truth.

Let me say that again in another way:

LIES that become YOUR truth = False narratives

I mentioned earlier that when a person deals with a trauma, crisis or difficult situation, their world flips upside down and suddenly, what was THEIR normal feels so very abnormal. We can also carry false narratives or past experiences from our childhood into our present and unconsciously accept it as our truth. We become so used to living in that false narrative that we may even believe that it is an actual truth. Negative experiences can flip your very core identity on its head! So, as you begin to take brave steps towards truth and healing, you must *feed the REAL reality.*

One of the false narratives I believed was that I was a hard-liner and very hard to live with due to my high expectations. And because I had to pick up the slack of being the discipline enforcer with the kids and maintain integrity in our family business, that false narrative was reinforced.

Therefore, I believed that I was a hard-nose and too intense. It took quite a while after I was out of those situations to realize that I was in fact, a mercy driven, loving person.

Some of the false narratives that I have dealt with or counseled clients on are:

Complicated

Hard to love

Tyrannical

Just a "b*#@="

Not attractive enough

Not skinny enough

Not capable

Not intelligent enough

Not any fun

Too serious

Too demanding

Unaccomplished

Too strict

And the list goes on and on! It's important during the process of taking brave steps that you allow God to untangle the webs of false narratives and build back your authentic identity. As you focus on feeding the reality of what God's word says, it will be a mirror to show you the true reflection of who you are. Knowing WHOSE you are is the most important of all!

You might not feel it nor believe it (yet), but as someone who has accepted Jesus Christ as their Lord and Savior, you genuinely are royalty! He is the King of Kings and as His daughter you are a princess with royal destiny on your life! His Word is full of truth and promises that give us the absolute truth about who we really are. It does not matter what you have done, what has been done to you or any bad situation that has transpired in your life; you can build back to brave by meditating on the truth in God's Word.

Rise To Brave!

Today, go to my website at kathysmalley.com. Download your free AFFIRMATIONS. I want you to read the "I AM" Affirmations *OUT LOUD*. Yes, read them out loud and let your own ears hear it! It's important because you are retraining your brain and feeding the real reality. As your real reality grows, the false narratives will come down. False narratives must come down for you to truly heal and flourish.

After reading the affirmations, ask the Holy Spirit to reveal to you one false narrative (lie/lies) that you have believed. Write it down, whether it is a lie about yourself, your future, your identity, etc and use a Scripture (feel free to use one from the list on my website) to replace the lie with the truth.

"And you did not receive "the spirit of religious duty", leading you back into the fear of never being good enough, but you have received the Spirit of full acceptance, enfolding you into the family of God. And you will never feel orphaned, for as He rises up within us, our spirits join Him in saying the words of tender affection, "Beloved Father". For the Holy Spirit makes God's fatherhood real to us as He whispers into our innermost being, "You are God's beloved child!"

Romans 8:15

6

MIRACULOUS MORNING

"The steadfast love of the Lord never ceases;
*His mercies never come to an end; **they are new***
every morning; great is your faithfulness.
"The Lord is my portion," says my soul,
"therefore I will hope in him."

LAMENTATIONS 3:22-23

*T*here is something miraculous about mornings and the first hours of the day. I know all of you night owls are already sighing at that first sentence! Yet I want to encourage you to rethink and reframe your mornings.

I get asked so often, "How did you increase your faith during your healing season?" The truth is, "Through a simplistic and consistent morning routine." Today, I want to show you how to simply create a morning routine and practically *do* it. I promise you it is a game-changer, whether you are a morning person *or* a night person!

His mercies are new every morning. I find it interesting that the Bible says His mercies are new every *morning*, but not every night. God is always with us and teaching us even as we sleep (Psalm 16:7); but there is something miraculous about the morning and the first start of the day. There is something about giving our day, our gratitude, our thinking, our bodies to Him at the very beginning of each day.

What did I do to build my faith? How did I burst through fear? How did I tackle the strain of managing four kids as a single mom? I want to emphasize it again—I literally got into a morning routine. I understand what it means to fight the depression and anxiety that trauma brings. It will not be easy, but don't make it so complex! God knows the season you are in, and He is there to help you as you take a brave step into establishing your miraculous morning!

There are five practical things you can do to glean the miraculous from your morning. Doing these five things consistently and intentionally will move you toward your brave and fearless self.

1. Gratitude journaling

2. Moving your body

3. Meditate on the Word

4. Declarations over yourself and life

5. Drink water and pray

Before you feel overwhelmed (yes, even doing one thing sometimes feels like a lot when life has so drastically been flipped upside down for you), let me put your mind at ease. Too many women get caught up thinking there is so much to do for their healing! It becomes overwhelming, so they do nothing at all. Or maybe things feel so chaotic or abnormal that you just don't know where to start. That's what this day's devotional is about — a simple place to start, small baby steps that ultimately will truly make a difference.

The first thing I do when I wake up is write in my Gratitude Journal. In my season of despair, I simply wrote 3 things down. I did it daily and soon found myself thinking and saying things I was grateful for during the day. Gratitude shifts everything for good. One book that I read on gratitude was *A Thousand Gifts* by Ann Voscamp. It set me on a path to a grateful heart and before long, I was "addicted" to journaling my gratitudes.

Second, every single day, move your body! This doesn't mean you have to work out for an hour at the gym or even at home. Just move! Moving your body might be marching around your house for 5 minutes, doing a few jumping jacks or dancing! Yes, put some Christian music on and be silly! You may not feel like it, but I promise it will bring some freedom to your soul. However, you move, just do it because it is significant to elevating serotonin in your body.

Third, put the Word of God in you! Oh ladies, this is imperative. You don't have to sit down and read the Bible for an hour, or dive into a Bible study (if you do, great!). As I was healing from trauma, I literally wrote Scriptures on 3 x 5 cards. I wrote one a day and read it out loud over and over. The Word of God is alive and actively changes the atmosphere internally and externally (Hebrews 4:12). Put on a Bible app that reads the Word out loud while you do your hair or get dressed. Listen to a devotional on your phone. Put the Word in you and watch it work. The Word of God is so powerful to heal you. See the "Scriptures for 31 Days to Brave" I have on my website kathysmalley.com to get you started.

Fourthly, speak declarations over your life. I have a tab for "Affirmations" on my website for your convenience. Declare who God says you are. As a side note, it may be awkward speaking out things that aren't reality yet but do it anyway! Call those things that are not as though they were (Romans 4:17)! One of the simple declarations that I do every day is, "Lord, I thank You for the good gift you are going to give me today. I'm going to be looking for it!" The Father God longs to lavish good gifts on us as His children and He has an unlimited source to do so. I say that every day and I see the multitude of blessings each day, whether it's a kind word or deed. God is so faithful.

Last, drink water and pray. Lol, I know that telling you to drink water is elementary, but I'm being serious. Cut down on the sugary drinks (or completely out if you can) and put lots of H2O in your body throughout the day and you will notice an increase in clarity and energy. I would sit out 6 water bottles on my island in the morning to help me stay on track.

Also, pray! Talk to God. Many times, we make prayer too complicated. Sometimes, my prayers were literally, "God, help." He longs for you to just be honest with Him. He already knows anyway and longs to commune with you. Just talk to Him, He is always listening and wants to have that intimacy with you.

It's amazing how many are now speaking about the science behind what God has already said. God created the body to heal itself, the brain can heal itself and the Word of God can spiritually heal you. However, we must come into alignment and use the resources and information that God has given us. We, as women, must get better about self-care. Give yourself the freedom and grace to not stay in a martyr attitude while giving out in exhaustion to others. Let the Holy Spirit lead you to "fill your own cup" and then overflow to others.

————————— *Rise To Brave!* —————————

So, I challenge you, "Do you have a morning routine?" I don't know about you; I want to grab a hold of His new mercies every morning. As you take these simple brave steps, God will meet you exactly where you are. There is no pressure or performance in this, but an understanding that your strength comes from your intimacy with Him; and as you consistently do it whether you feel like it or not, you are partnering with the God of the universe who lavishly loves you and will make you whole.

Take 5 minutes today:

1. Write down 3 things you are grateful for in your life.

2. Walk, march or dance to music.

3. Read the Scripture at the end of this chapter and ask the Holy Spirit to speak to you.

4. Go to my website and read the I AM Affirmations over yourself.

5. Drink a glass of water and talk to God.

Ask the Holy Spirit to help you to be consistent every day.

"Every good and perfect gift is from above, coming down from the Father of lights, with whom there is no variation or shadow due to change."

James 1:17

1

A COUCH IN COLORADO

I sat with my knees draped over the beautiful blue velvet sofa in the hotel restaurant bar where we were staying. My husband had made the decision to come to a Colorado treatment center for his addiction and healing. I felt hopeful, but exhausted. I had been sitting there for some time deep in thought. I gazed out the window, watching the snowflakes consistently falling like magic from the sky. This was what I had fought for and prayed would happen—and now we were here. As I watched the snow fall, a borage of unexpected thoughts came softly flooding into my mind.

"What if my husband *actually* GOT his healing?"

"What if he *did* heal and I didn't?"

I felt nauseous as the questions taunted my mind.

Before you judge me or misunderstand what was going on, let me say... I LOVED this man! I had fought a thousand rounds for this man! I *believed* in this man for 25+ years! And now we were at yet another program, hoping that this was the restoration I had longed for my husband to find. I was fully hoping. I was committed to victory, yet in that moment the reality shook me. I felt a different anxiety and fear that un-corked a different emotion. I didn't know what it was like to *not* fight for him. I had been so focused on *his* addictions and his healing to focus on anything else.

As soon as the questions entered my mind, I felt an intense tug on my heart from the Lord. It was like my questions echoed through the quiet room and I *knew* God wanted to answer them. Ever so sweetly, I felt the Lord's still small voice whisper to me,

"Kathy, it doesn't matter what *he* does. Just trust Me."

Little did I know that this would be a pivotal moment and set me on course to genuine wholeness. Instantly, something rose up inside me; something foreign that I had not ever felt. My next thought kind of shocked me, "Over my dead body am I not healing!"

There was this fierceness that began to bubble up inside of me. The thoughts began to race, "I WILL HEAL. No matter what."

Up until that minute, I had been in full survival mode. So much shock. So many ugly revelations of sin. So much drama and fear. So much pain. Minutes, hours and days of desperation to see my husband get the help he needed. I had rallied in the trauma to hold my family and my kids together and believe for what seemed impossible. Yet in all the madness, one small decision had not truly registered in my brain. I needed to heal. I didn't just *need* to… I *had* to heal! And on that couch in Colorado, I realized there was NO WAY I would only see him heal and not do the same for myself! Yes, he had chosen very destructive paths and left utter devastation in the wake of his choices. It was true that he had so much to untangle and intense work to do for his healing. However, right there, the Holy Spirit prompted me to shift my focus off of what my husband did. I also had been through so much and the wounds ran deep. And Jesus was not talking to me about my husband… He was talking to me about me and *my* healing.

We had come to the treatment center in Colorado for my husband to find healing and wholeness. Yet alone in that quiet reflective space, God moved my heart and I felt myself throw down the proverbial gauntlet,

"Yes, I will heal—no matter what it takes."

And I meant it.

It was a simple scene and a simple moment. But that moment changed everything in my journey to healing. *I* made a choice. *I* drew a line in the sand. *I had* to heal, come hell or high water!

Did it happen overnight? Absolutely not, but I believe it was a definitive crossroad for me. Did I know what to do? No, not at all! But I had decided and now the stake was in the ground. I believe God reset my compass on that lovely blue sofa in Colorado, and even though I was worn and weary, I decided to heal.

Maybe you are at a crossroad in your life. Maybe you have been fighting the good fight to see victory in your family, your finances, your dreams/future or your health! Maybe your focus has been on a spouse, a child coming home, a new job. Maybe you have been in "fix it" mode with a child's behavior problem or a friend's betrayal. You may have fought hard to believe, encourage, and pray for someone or a situation that needs restoration and healing. Yet I think sometimes it's so easy to focus on the problem or the situation and forget that the only person we can change is ourselves! Change in every situation or circumstance starts with us finding our own wholeness and healing. Where is your gaze? Are you focused on a circumstance and missing the beauty of the Lord gently ministering to you... about you? Is there a line you need to draw in the sand? A stake you need to put in the ground? It doesn't matter if it's a life- altering trauma or an exhaustion from giving out to everyone around you. There is truth to leaning into Jesus to hear Him gently say, "It doesn't matter what they do. Let's deal with what is wounded/hurting you and/or keeping you from being all you can be." Healing is a choice. It really is a place of surrendering to trust God. Healing is trusting that He will deal with them or the situation and trusting Him enough to let Him minister healing and wholeness in us.

———— *Rise To Brave* ————

Take a few minutes and write down a few people or situations that you need to give to God:

_____

_____

_____

Pray out loud and physically cup your hands as you picture lifting the person(s) or situation(s) to God: Lord, I want to heal. I want to give _____ to You. I set my gaze upon You and I trust You because I know You are trustworthy. I commit to let You heal my heart, no matter what it takes. Thank You for strengthening my will to choose to heal. Holy Spirit show me the way to go and give me the courage to make each step as You lead and guide me to victory. In Jesus' name. Amen.

"O Lord, my healing God, I cried out for help (a miracle) and you healed me."

Psalm 30:2 TPT

9

BLUE STICKY NOTE

I remember sitting at the desk in my study. The house was remarkably quiet, not that it wasn't normal, especially as the kids weren't there. The kids had just left for school after the morning frenzy of making breakfast, packing lunches, calling them down the stairs 14 times or searching for the missing item of the day. Typically, today it was my youngest daughter's spandex shorts which she needed for her school uniform skirt that seemed to disappear into the abyss of her closet overnight. "Hugs and love" I would always say as they headed out the door. This gesture was non-negotiable in the family; I made it mandatory that they hug each other and say "I love you" before leaving to go anywhere. That tradition was put into play after my brother was tragically killed in a car accident. And trust me, boys need to know and experience physical affection! And no side hugs! This mama required the full "squeeze you, love you" kind of hug. Physical touch changes the chemistry inside your kids, but that's another conversation for another day.

Some days, by the time the kids had left flying out the door with lunches in tow, I felt as if I already needed a nap! But after they left, every morning I would go into my study. At one time it had been "our study", but since the divorce, it had become fully mine. It became my sanctuary of peace, a quiet place where God began to show me how to step into the brave woman He had created me to be. It was in that room (that had once been defiled by pornography and numerous fights about money and secrets) that I recreated a space to connect with God to experience His healing and redeeming love. That's what God does, you know? He takes the pain and places we feel betrayed or hurt and turns them into opportunities of praise and position. Creating a beautiful new space of expectation and communion with God was the beginning of coming out of my grief and into a place that I would be forever changed.

The house was always so quiet whenever the kids left, and for the first few minutes, I would feel an immense loneliness and the unbearable weight of my story would come crashing in…. It was daunting and scary sitting in that room alone at times, and many mornings, the tears would pour… but I will never forget this one day. Day 1. The day I made a decision to set a new future in motion. I sat at my desk, staring at a stack of blue sticky notes, lost somewhere in my thoughts (the grief cycle at work again). Suddenly, an inner knowing awakened in my spirit. I knew at that moment God was working all things for my good, despite the embarrassment and shame I felt at the thought of others learning of my story. Not some, not a little, but ALL. He was working all things for my good and nothing would be wasted. I grabbed a pen and wrote out my first declaration.

"I will share my story from a stage, no matter how hard,
and deal hope to others"

So, I began my journey to be brave, on a single blue sticky note. I made a decision back in 2016 to take God as His word. Even though everything in my life looked impossible, I decided to believe that even in the room where I felt betrayed and dishonored, God was with me in this, and He would work ALL of it for my good. There was a resolve that day, no matter what He asked me to do, no matter how scary, embarrassing, hard or long, I was latching on to His promise for myself, my daughters, my sons, and all the women coming behind me. So, the commitment was set that day, in the very midst of my mess when everything looked bleak, that I would share my story of His redeeming love so others would have hope out of their own devastating grief.

———— *Rise To Brave!* ————

We all have a story. It takes raw, real grit, faith and courage to believe God will work all of our trials and traumas for our good. It takes even more courage to tell others about it. So today, it is your turn to be brave. Pull out a sticky note, a 3 x 5 card, a big 8 x11 piece of paper, or heck, even write it in lipstick on your bathroom mirror. Whatever works for you, just write it down. Decide and dare to believe God, that He has a redeeming story for you as well. Write your declaration down and know today that your pain matters! Put it in writing that you will bravely share it one day with someone who needs a hand to pull them up. Get a pen and jump into your brave journey!

"I will share my story, no matter how hard,
and give hope to another. "

"We know that all things work together for good to those who love God."

Romans 8:28

9

REWIRE YOUR BRAIN

*W*hen we are experiencing a life-altering trauma (car accidents, natural disasters, physical violence, and betrayal); our brains stop functioning like they normally do. We enter survival mode, kind of like a deer in headlights when there is an immediate threat. When we are in normal life mode, we can shift back out of a threatening situation and function normally.

However, when we are in trauma, particularly one resulting from broken relationships, it changes the way we think, act and feel. When one is in trauma, the "deer in headlights" response doesn't fade away, but it sticks with us. The constant intrusive thoughts don't just go away without work. There are many ways the interrupted synapses can be reversed, and one is by rewiring the brain. When you look at an MRI of a traumatized brain, you can visually see the differences in synapses; it's almost like the surface of the moon with huge divots in it. When we consistently do the healing work, we can actually "rewire" our brains back to their original healthy design.

Understanding the difference between *Ego-ship* vs. *Ownership* helped me to bravely walk out my healing. When we operate in *Ego-ship*, we are relying on our own ability to protect ourselves rather than trusting God. It is a form of self-sustaining and self-reliance. When we walk in *Ownership*, we choose to acknowledge that "I am in control of accessing the healing that God has already paid for me to have." I came to realize that I must partner with God, take brave steps consistently, and walk out my healing. Several concepts may be repeated from different devotional aspects because they are that important! These simple steps that God led me to do and share are scientifically proven to help the traumatized brain. Science is just now catching up with what the Bible has said for thousands of years.

Many of the simplistic steps done in repetition will help you to rewire your brain after trauma. Meditation, gratitude-journaling, moving your body (3 thirty-minute walks a week improve clinical depression), journaling and doing random acts of kindness literally cause chemical changes in your brain's neural pathways.

As I transitioned in my healing, I realized that consistency of these rituals done at morning and night were the catalyst to becoming my best brave version of myself. Did I feel like doing them consistently? No, not every time. However, as a believer and a therapist, I knew the truth of God's Word and I knew the truth behind the science. The truth was that if I continued to do the rituals every day, and I acted in faith knowing I already possessed everything inside of me for healing, my healing HAD to happen. I realized that if I just did it afraid, or when I didn't want to, or despite how I felt—my traumatized brain WOULD HEAL. So, I kept doing it— regardless. I know how hard it is to commit. Believe me, I do! But as you slowly add in each brave step, you are establishing your desire and identity and rewiring your brain for victory!

If you find yourself without a morning routine, just start somewhere! One of the first things I incorporated was a simple five-minute walk (more like a stroll around my backyard) and writing just three gratitudes. I did it whether or not I cried all the way through it.

The victory will come. Start somewhere. Stay consistent. Don't give up. Remember, it is PROVEN that the activities I listed above will help rewire your brain. Yes, you should have a good therapist after experiencing trauma and they can guide you into things such as EMDR, neurofeedback, and other techniques that can further help. But the daily consistent rituals are powerfully brave and impactful. They will work with anxiety, depression, negative thoughts or wrong thinking.

Rise to Brave!

Which of these activities are you doing consistently every day? (Circle all that apply):

Prayer/Meditation

Gratitude Journaling (lists of things you are grateful for)

Moving Your Body

Random Acts of Kindness

Reading God's Word

If you haven't incorporated any of these activities into your daily routine, make a commitment to do them, even if it's in the simplest of form. Ask the Holy Spirit for the desire to walk out the steps towards rewiring your brain.

"And let us not grow weary of doing good, for in due season we will reap, if we do not give up."

Galatians 6:9

16

STEP UP TO THE PLATE
AND SWING

"The cave you fear to enter holds the treasures you seek…"
–JOSEPH CAMPBELL

*Y*ou have a dream inside your heart. You want to start a business, write a book, go back to school, lead a Bible study, run a 5K, lose 20 pounds…. And the list is endless. There has been something that consistently pops up that you want to do but are afraid to put it out there and begin. Many times, we think we need to know more, learn more, practice more, have our schedule streamlined, put our home in order, and organize our life. Life will always be busy, there will never be a time when we have it all together, and hell is not going to freeze over!

God knew the plan and purpose for your life before you were even born and the only person who can hold us back from the epic accomplishments He ordained for us is ourselves. I want to remind you of the story of David and Goliath.

Most of us probably remember hearing about the shepherd boy, David fighting the giant, Goliath. We know David defeated Goliath, but I want to share a couple of things about the story that God showed me that helped me start two new businesses, open my heart to love again, and allowed me to move past my fear of failing.

Goliath was a fierce warrior who is recorded to have stood over 9 feet tall and was covered in stellar armor from his head to toe. He was taunting the armies of Israel day in and day out for someone to step up and fight him. All the men who saw him were afraid.

David was a young shepherd boy who merely tended to sheep and one day he overheard the threats of the giant. Disgusted, he went to the King to tell him that he would fight and defeat the giant. King Saul made it clear that he did not believe David had what it took to defeat Goliath. He reminded him that he didn't have the size, experience, or physical strength to defeat the giant. David was not deterred.

Here is what I want you to really pay attention to: David had not been through warrior training, he didn't wait to have custom made armor, he didn't require the approval of others, and he did not believe it was all up to him to be successful. You know what he did? He simply PICKED UP THE RESOURCES HE HAD, a sling and 5 stones, belief in God, and he stepped up to the plate, aimed at the target and saved his entire homeland that day. What if you stopped waiting to have it all together, to learn more, prepare more or wait more and simply start with the resources God has already given you and step up to the plate of your destiny? David was the least likely to be chosen, he had not fought a war before or killed an average sized man, much less a Giant champion. The only difference between him and all the other men was deciding to go for it and knowing God would help him. David was a person just like you and me. God had a plan and a purpose for him before he was born. Fear could have kept him from stepping up to the plate of his destiny that day, but he decided to use what He did have and trust God with the rest. The action he took that day was the beginning of him becoming known as the 'man after God's own heart'. What if you stopped hesitating, stopped making excuses, or stopped allowing others' opinions to influence you or cause you to shrink back? What if you picked up the resources you have and went for it?

I had been praying about a new business idea that would allow me to pass something onto my kids with their own last name attached to it. After losing our family business that all four of my kids felt some pride and ownership in, I had this desire in my heart to create something else they could be part of if they wanted to. I felt God nudging me to learn about real estate investing. A weekend conference popped up in my social media feed and I immediately signed up to go. I listened and learned for 3 full days, and they offered a coaching program to help you get started. I jumped in and signed up that weekend. On the very next day, I started putting together the LLC to start a business in real estate with no license and no prior experience. Ford (my children's last name) Acquisitions, LLC was born. It was messy, it wasn't perfect, and I had no idea what I was doing. But I decided to go for it without having it all together and without prior training or experience of any kind. I had the determination and motivation to do the work, I had been successful in other businesses I had launched, and I trusted God. Within the very first 12 months of that business, God blessed the growth to over 6 figures of profit and multiple 6 figures the second year. I know, I know, women of faith don't really talk about the money they make. But, it's interesting that God chose (in the Bible) to highlight that the esteemed "Proverbs 31 Woman" made good money of her own so she could take care of her family as well as give back to others! Money is a resource and in the hand of a kingdom minded woman, we can help fund every good work our heart desires and spread the love of Jesus!

And you know what else?! My two sons decided to join that business and begin their own journey in real estate because God gave me the courage to step up in faith and do it anyway—even though I was scared.

——————— *Rise To Brave!* ———————

It may not be a business, but you have something you want to do that you haven't begun yet. Maybe it's even a dream that has been tucked away and dormant in your heart for a very long time. Whatever it is, it is time to pick up the resources you have and do something. Don't panic! I am not going to require you to wake up tomorrow and form the LLC or announce on your social media that you are hiking Kilimanjaro or starting back to school. (Of course, you absolutely can do that if you want!)

Today's rise to brave step is to simply open your computer and begin to *research* about it. If you want to lose weight, start researching different options, or if you know you want to go to a gym and get a trainer, begin researching about trainers and gyms in your area. Maybe you want to serve at your church in a leadership role, get online and start looking at the different ways to get involved.

Whatever it is, it is time to go for it! Don't wait; pick up the resources you have, step up to the plate, and swing, girlfriend, SWING!

"Delight yourself in the Lord, and He will give you the desires of your heart."

Psalm 37:4

||

DANCE THE BLUES AWAY

*W*hen you experience severe stress or trauma, some details are not at the forefront of your mind. Many days are a blur and other days feel like you're walking in the winds of a hurricane. On other days, just getting your clothes on and out the door is a big task and major accomplishment! After the initial shock of my husband's addiction and affairs, I committed to going back to the gym; this was a huge decision for me initially. I had always worked out and found it to be a de-stressor and a place of solace for me. I went back to the gym because I had longed to be back in a rhythm, of any kind. To say it was haphazard at first would be an understatement.

I walked into the gym one day feeling very proud of myself that I had woke up, jumped into the car and into the gym (with my legs shaved of course, because I hate the feeling of yoga pants on my unshaved legs-lol)! I was feeling accomplished before I even worked out. Suddenly I noticed that people were staring at me. My first thoughts were I had a sign on my forehead that stated what was going on in my life. *Why were people looking at me?* I decided it didn't matter because I was winning simply by being there. After about thirty minutes, my trainer (bless his sweet heart) came over and said "Kathy, you might want to go to the locker room and check your leggings." *What?* I looked down and my solid black yoga pants were inside out! I was mortified. Remind you, I had been squatting and bending over all around the gym for 30 minutes. Geez. I ran into the locker room to fix the ridiculousness. I'd love to say that was the only time I found myself in that type of situation, but it was one of many in that season. Has anyone else ever driven along the highway while lost in your thoughts and completely missed your exit? Maybe you can relate!

All to say, during that time of fresh trauma, my head was in the clouds on numerous occasions, but I still made a decision to "move". Even though the first steps of getting my body moving again were difficult; the endorphins that it released helped me feel better instantly. Endorphins interact with the receptors in your brain and reduce your perception of pain (Isn't God's body/brain design amazing?) Endorphins also trigger a positive feeling in your body! Moderate exercise is proven to be more effective than an antidepressant and can radically shift your energy, increase clarity and focus, and boost your overall mood. I decided to move my body every day no matter what. It became a daily non-negotiable and catapulted my healing physically and emotionally. It can do the same for you! The great thing about exercise is it can reap immediate rewards with just 10-15 minutes of time. If you really want to feel better, whether you are in the middle of deep grief or the occasional down feelings or low energy, this one commitment can give back more long-term benefits than any pill or vacation ever will.

Exercises that involve cross movement and engage both arms and legs- such as walking, running, swimming, weight training or dancing – are some of the best choices to begin to try. I loved that I was more in control of my mental health than ever before. If I began to feel anxious or felt a crash coming on in the afternoon, I could literally throw tennis shoes on and go for a walk/run or jump on a stationary bike with loud music and immediately shift my mood and have a keener sense of clarity. I walked out of that hard place in my life and began to start new businesses and face other decisions where I needed to be sharp and focused; again, exercise was the key to increased mental strength. I want to encourage you today to "move your body". Depression and anxiety make us want to curl up in a ball and close the world out forever. It is a brave step to move your physical body regularly. It may start with walking for only 5 minutes, or doing 10 jumping jacks, but when you get up and move it will change your body chemistry. It will help you walk out of the hopelessness, depression and anxiety as well as maximize your mental stamina to accomplish your goals and dreams. I understand what it takes to exert yourself physically in times of stress; but it is such an incredibly important step! This is moving forward in your journey! It may seem hard to begin, but the action is simple, and it will be imperative to your emotional wellness! I challenge you today to reach deep inside you and commit to start moving your body every day. Lean in my sweet sister, just begin with 10 minutes of exercise, and watch how the power that made the body will begin to heal the body. Women all over the world are taking back control of their mental health with these simple steps that build on each other one brave day at a time.

The words of the writer Paul in Philippians 3:13-14 are encouraging,

> *"Brothers and sisters, I do not consider myself yet*
> *to have taken hold of it. But one thing I do; forgetting*
> *what is behind and straining toward what is ahead,*
> *"I press on toward the goal to win the prize for which*
> *God has called me heavenward in Christ Jesus."*

Be encouraged! Press on sister, press on.

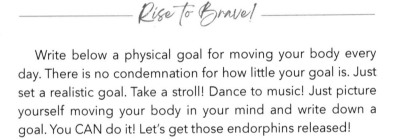

——————— *Rise To Brave!* ———————

Write below a physical goal for moving your body every day. There is no condemnation for how little your goal is. Just set a realistic goal. Take a stroll! Dance to music! Just picture yourself moving your body in your mind and write down a goal. You CAN do it! Let's get those endorphins released!

I will _____ for _____minutes every day. (It might even help you to set a specific time.)

"I can do all things through Christ who gives me strength!"

Philippians 4:13

12

THE MIRACLE IN YOUR MOUTH

I bet I heard myself thinking these words hundreds of times, and saying it out loud often… "I'm so overwhelmed."

The other phrase that seemed to be constantly coming out of my mouth when well-meaning friends would ask me how I was doing, "It's a lot." I thought that response was better than regurgitating all the sad, awful details. I felt I was being non-bitter with that phrase. The truth was that I did feel overwhelmed, and it was honestly A LOT. Yet, one day I came across a scripture that changed my life and helped me create a new story:

> *"God rewrote the text of my life when I*
> *opened the book of my heart to His eyes"*
> 2 Samuel 22:25

I remember reading that and feeling the words literally imprint on inside of me, God can rewrite the text of my life … "God can rewrite the text of my life!!" I needed my life to be rewritten! I realized in that moment, that I could partner with God and change the story I had created with my wrong talk and belief systems. Do you know you are your best salesman? You sell yourself on your own narrative or story every single day. When God gave me a word that promised He would rewrite the text of my life, it was as though someone had given my drowning heart a lifeline of hope. I just had to look at it differently. I may have felt overwhelmed, my finances may have been depleted, but I discovered that the more I spoke that out, the more it validated and created that part of my story. When I opened my heart to what God saw, it changed my perspective! I was capable, I was resourceful, and I was loved. I began to allow God to speak into my life and rewrite a new story and it started with what I said out of my mouth.

I will not lie and say that it was easy, that wouldn't be truthful. Yet I asked the Lord to help flip my script, so that I could speak the things that aligned with the victorious future I desired. I began to disempower the old stories I was feeling and reframe my thinking and words.

According to the National Science Foundation, an average person has about 12,000 to 60,000 thoughts per day. Of those, 80% are negative thoughts. It is also said (John Gottman and Robert Levenson's published work) that it takes five positive comments to counteract a negative one.

No wonder Paul tells us in 2 Corinthians 10:5 to take our thoughts captive! So often, many self- sabotage their futures with negative thoughts and words. We are the righteousness of Christ (2 Corinthians 5:21), but we talk like paupers—especially to ourselves!

As you move forward in your healing, one of the most important truths to acknowledge is that "you take you everywhere you go." That sounds so obvious, but we must understand that our thoughts and words can be our most damning hurdle. The only way to change the narrative of your thoughts is to do the work to change them. If you are constantly thinking things like,

It's a lot.

I'm always going to be alone.

I'll never get married.

I'll never get a good job.

I'll never lose weight.

I'll never feel happy again.

Then guess what? You will draw those negative things to you. Even when it seems dumb or sounds silly, speak out the positive truth based on God's Word and begin creating a new future! Sometimes you will literally have to bully your own thoughts. Praying, meditating, and reading Scripture out loud, journaling, and declaring affirmations over your life will begin to counteract the negative narratives that haunt your mind. (Feel free to download my affirmations from www. kathysmalley.com)

You may know and find the answers and truths, but it can be hard to accept them. This takes consistency and commitment to do it. I know how hard it is, but I promise you it will transform you to another level. If we deny the truth, we simply can't go to the next level of transformation in our lives. This entire concept is the truth that is found in God's Word:

"Stop imitating the ideals and opinions of the culture around you but be inwardly transformed by the Holy Spirit through a total reformation of how you think.

*This will empower you to discern God's will as you live a
beautiful life, satisfying and perfect in His eyes."*
Romans 12:2

WOW. Isn't it incredible to know that getting rid of negative thoughts and words can change your life? That is true motivation to bravely switch the narrative and use your mouth to create miracles!

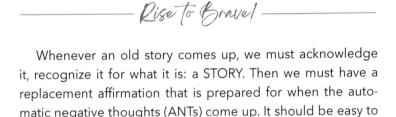

Whenever an old story comes up, we must acknowledge it, recognize it for what it is: a STORY. Then we must have a replacement affirmation that is prepared for when the automatic negative thoughts (ANTs) come up. It should be easy to remember and in present tense.

Example:
Story: "I am overwhelmed and I don't have the time
            or money to live the life I want."
New Truth: "I am resourceful, capable and I find the time
            and resources to support my dreams."

Story: "I'm not worthy of abundance in relationships
            or my career."
New Truth: "I am worthy of love and success and Jesus
            came to give me an abundant life."

Story: "I am afraid of what others may think."
New Truth: "I am confident, uniquely designed, and divinely appointed."
            "I do not fear, but have a spirit of love, power,
            and a sound mind."

I recognize the story I keep telling myself… (Insert the negative thought/words you fight)

_____

_____

_____

I choose to see and speak this differently … I AM… (Insert affirmation)

_____

_____

_____

"God rewrote the text of my life when I opened the books of my heart to His eyes"

2 Samuel 22:25

13

BETRAYAL

Betrayal is among the most devastating losses a person can experience. This kind of loss happens in so many ways and it can affect you deeply. Wherever it comes from and whatever form it takes, it can cause great suffering. When we've been betrayed, we go through many emotional stages. Initially, you may experience some level of shock and then you may face multiple emotions such as anger, depression, disbelief and sometimes, denial. I think one of the hardest things to do is accepting that it *WILL* hurt. I'd describe it as feeling like your soul has been ripped into pieces. Embracing the pain, acknowledging what has happened, and feeling all the feelings will allow you to move through it and not stay stuck in that place of paralyzing pain. Betrayal hits your core, your very soul and staying stuck in it would be destructive. The irony of betrayal is that when you are betrayed, you sometimes end up betraying yourself. That is the worst betrayal of all! So, how do we bravely move forward in the face of betrayal?

I have experienced a deep level of betrayal and there was one huge motivating factor that led me to choose to be brave and decide to heal: the pain of remaining the same, stuck in the mire of betrayal and trauma was greater than the fear of change. I realized that although I hurt and ached and experienced so many emotions, I did not want to be this way forever. I had a desire for change and an identity I could grab a hold of through Jesus Christ and the power of the Holy Spirit.

As I processed the betrayal of my husband; I realized I had also been betrayed by someone else—myself! Self-betrayal would actually be the betrayal that would keep me from being free if I didn't recognize it and address it. What do I mean by self-betrayal? I wasn't taking care of myself in this traumatic pain. I wasn't taking care of my physical body; I wasn't nurturing the truths of identity that I knew Christ had for me. In essence, self-betrayal is denying opportunities and growth for myself because of mistakes I had made in my grief. I was buying into the shame from choices I had made in my pain. I was denying myself the things that were my God-given and endorsed right! God sent His Son, Jesus, so that I could be loved, seen and known! That was my God-given inheritance! We also self-betray when we deny our needs/wants in order to be accepted by others, for example, saying "yes" when we want to say "no". We *enable* instead of *confronting*. We allow others to violate our boundaries. Sometimes, self-betrayal is demanding something from a spouse that they can't give and only God can do!

When I chose to truly forgive my husband for violating my trust and confidence through betrayal; I found freedom and I had to get honest before God about my own self-betrayal. The Father was so tender in teaching me that indeed He had paid a high price for my inheritance through Jesus on the cross. That everything I desired (being seen, loved and known) was already mine through Jesus. I began to believe God's truths about my identity and realized that affirmation, forgiveness (towards others and myself) and freedom were my new normal.

Although betrayal is excruciating, I can honestly say now that there was beauty that came from the ashes of the betrayal in my life—I found myself again and my identity was redefined in that season of brokenness. If you break down the word RE-DE-FINED... you can see the implication that truly moved me forward into my future. Let this season be a season of re-FIND- ing YOU! As you navigate towards a brave new future and the pain of betrayal feels crippling, ask the Holy Spirit to give you a redefining of yourself and the life you long for. Let the Holy Spirit show you what Christ died for you to have! Then partner with Jesus to bravely walk forward into all He has for you!

Rise To Brave!

This may be hard for some of you because we are so programmed to think we must "earn" our blessings! Today, I want you to take your time and write out what a perfect day for you would be! Start from the time you wake up, until you go to bed. What would you be doing? Who would you be with? Where would you be? How would you feel? No limitations and no explanations. Let your imagination flow and enjoy it with the Holy Spirit. Do not skip this step. This is a brave exercise and there is power in creating a vision of what you long for. Write out the details of the desires in your heart while beginning to understand that God has so much good in store for you!

"The thief comes only to steal and kill and destroy. I have come that they may have life and have it in all its fullness."

John 10:10 ESV

14

A BIBLE AND A BIKINI

"Come along with me..."
SONG OF SOLOMON 2:10

"Draw near to Him and He will draw near ...
(or take leaps) toward you."
JAMES 4:8

I grew up with five siblings, two brothers and three sisters. My life was full of built-in playmates and people all the time. My dad was one of nine kids, so family gatherings and holidays were often large and loud. I never knew quiet or quaint and was most comfortable with colossal chaos and that pretty much described what growing up was like for me. I loved the fullness of home, the crazy busyness in the kitchen during the holidays and birthdays, and all the noise of the normal day-to-day life. I think I genuinely thought fighting was an official love language! Our family vacations were no different. All eight of us would pile into the family RV and travel all over the country in tight quarters sharing beds and bathrooms and fighting over who got which small box of the old time multi-pack of mini cereals my mom never forgot to pack. Being alone wasn't a part of my childhood. And after high school, I went straight to college and into marriage, and then we had four kids in five years which left life continuing in a pattern full of people.

Relationships are amazing. We need connection. God created us for connection. He also longs for us to know what it is to be still in Him… alone. As women, moms, daughters, friends, leaders, entrepreneurs, sisters… we often find ourselves and our identity in our relationships.

There is nothing wrong with that and it can be amazing—unless we lose ourselves along the way. Too many times we don't take the time alone to get away and get with God. It was no different for me until life was turned upside down and I found myself suddenly thrust into being alone. This day may stretch you and it may be a little uncomfortable, but it's time to find you again.

I knew I needed to get away and try to come up for air from the smothering grief that was holding me down. I had never been on a trip all by myself, ever. I jumped online and started searching for a flight and booked a trip to Newport Beach in California for just one passenger. Just me, on a flight alone, at a hotel on a beach I had never been to before for five days. I was desperate to hear God and find myself again. So, I figured I needed a Bible, a bikini and a huge stack of brave! I needed to turn off the world, so I could hear from God in a time I was desperate for answers. Five days in a new place, walking beaches alone, eating every breakfast, lunch, and dinner alone, browsing shops alone, crawling in bed and waking alone—no phone, no talking, no texting. Just me and Jesus, alone. It was scary and dinners in nice restaurants were awkward. It took all the courage I could muster to go and leave my kids during a time when life was falling apart. Somehow, I found the strength.

That brave step to take a trip all alone, in a place I had never been, just to be with God would be a defining moment in my life that changed how I saw God and myself forever. I have not been the same ever since.

Rise To Brave!

Today, it is time for you to pick one thing that you have never done alone before and do it. Turn off the phone and push yourself out of your comfort zone.

Go to dinner alone. Go to a movie alone. Drive to a national park for the day, pack a lunch and just be alone. Something unfamiliar, somewhere you haven't been or something you haven't done before. Document your day(s) below to remember just how brave you are choosing to be!

_____

_____

_____

_____

_____

_____

_____

_____

_____

"Draw near to Him and HE will draw near ...(or take leaps) toward you."

James 4:8

15

AN ATTITUDE OF GRATITUDE

*A*s I walked through a dark night of my soul, I remember literally staring blankly at my bedroom wall and thinking, *"My life sucks."*

That's pretty blunt, but it was truly how I felt. I was knee-deep in sorrow, overwhelmed by debt, and drowning in thoughts about the implosion of my world. On top of my heavy heart, the car was in the shop, I had hives and the kids were struggling too. I didn't know where I was going to live nor how I was going to provide. It was hard to even get up and get the kids to school. I was mentally and emotionally exhausted and the weight of life was trying to consume me. The bottom line was that I was mad, sad, fearful and did NOT feel grateful. Gratitude was definitely not on my radar at that moment. But God…

I heard the Holy Spirit whisper to my heart,

In all circumstances, give thanks…

Honestly, I moaned out loud, "Yeah, right." Yet the Holy Spirit kept nudging me to look up the verse in 1 Thessalonians 5:16-18, so I did.

"*Lord, teach me to offer You a heart of thanksgiving and praise in all my daily experiences of life. Teach me to be joyful always, to pray continually and to give thanks in all my circumstances. I accept them as Your will for my life.*"

But how could I give thanks for being betrayed? How could I be grateful in the middle of the mess that my life was in right now? It seemed so impossible.

If you have been living long enough, I am sure you can relate. As a therapist, I knew there were scientific studies that revealed the power of gratitude. In fact, it has been documented that a one- time act of thoughtful gratitude (being thankful) produced an immediate 10% increase in happiness and 35% reduction in depressive symptoms. Wow. I love how science continues to validate God's Word! So, regardless of how I felt at that moment, I started implementing it as a daily practice.

I got out a piece of paper and was determined to think of things that I was grateful for and write them down. My mind was so cluttered with pain that it was genuinely hard at first. I decided I would not stop until I wrote at least ten things down.

My kids.

That I had food to eat.

The smell of freshly mowed grass.

My sisters

A fireplace burning on a cold day

And the list went on until I had listed ten things. *Somehow, I knew that gratitude would be a gateway to my healing and joy.* What I had begrudgingly started on that dismal day became a well of hope for me, as I decided to consistently do it every day.

After several days of recording the things I was grateful for, I noticed a critical inner voice running through my mind. For example, I wrote that I was grateful that I presently had a place to live. As I wrote that gratitude down, I immediately heard my inner critic saying, *"Not for long."*

That negative talk came from something I had overheard during my divorce that rattled me. Why did that thought keep popping into my head? My inner critic was trying to interfere with my feelings of gratitude and distort how I saw things; and of course, the devil did NOT like my pursuit of a grateful heart! After all, God instructed us to be grateful, and actually commanded it. Why? Because He knows that choosing to develop a spirit of gratitude will bring us sustained joy.

You might be asking "What do I have to be grateful for?" Perhaps focusing on what we are grateful *for* is the wrong approach. Most of the Scriptural references do not speak of gratitude *for* things but suggest an overall spirit or attitude of gratitude. Instead of just being thankful *for* things, we focus on being thankful in our circumstances—whatever they may be.

Gratitude is the gateway to your healing and breakthrough from fear. It unlocks our hearts and minds to a true joy that is eternal. Happiness is only temporary and circumstantial, whereas true joy doesn't require that circumstances be good or perfect. The Bible tells us that the joy of the Lord is our strength and gratitude can be the pathway that opens the true joy in our hearts.

During my journey, I became persistent and consistent at journaling my gratitude. Many days, all I could do was force myself to write a few down. Yet as time went on, I looked forward to my gratefulness journaling every morning. Little did I know just how powerful and impactful this mindfulness practice (and obedience to God's Word) would be. I truly believe it was the wind in my sails during the most turbulent times of my life. I got into such a wonderful rhythm of writing my gratitudes that I set a goal of writing out 1,000 things that I was grateful for in that season. I was determined to create a new life, so I bought a spiral notebook just for my list of gratitudes. I discovered there are 25 lines on each page in a standard spiral. I carried it everywhere with me so I could journal even simple things I found myself thankful for. I still have that notebook filled with my grateful heart and the one thousand lines that became a memoir of God's goodness and answered prayers.

Rise To Brave!

Today, start with writing one or ten things down in a notebook. If you have a separate journal or notebook, designate it as your "Gratitude Journal." Commit to simply writing in it every day; it will amaze you how it shifts your perspective. It may be the smell of freshly cut grass or that you can hear the birds in the sky. It doesn't matter what you are grateful for as long as you allow yourself to bravely build a grateful heart with an attitude of gratitude. Watch fear, shame, grief and past regret fall away as you begin to implement this one step.

"In everything give thanks: for this is God's will for you in Christ Jesus."

1 Thessalonians 5:18

16

NEVER ALONE

*I*t was yet another Friday night alone. My two kids that lived at home were busy with their school activities and were spending the night with friends. I decided to do what I had done quite a few nights in that season. I went to Target. I loved Target and there was just something soothing about walking and pushing my red shopping cart around the store. Honestly, I didn't always buy anything, but window shopping was somewhat therapeutic for me. I would peruse every section, looking at clothes, smelling the candles and even do lots of people watching.

Sometimes, I would see a happy couple and feel the angst in my gut and be flooded with memories. Inevitably, the thoughts would come, "why did my family have to suffer so much?" Many shopping trips, the tears would gently roll down my cheeks as I just strolled Target in an attempt to not feel so lonely. Yet, I often found myself lonely in the middle of a crowd.

That night was a tough one. I had struggled with loneliness all day. I had been in the store for an hour and finally just put my shopping cart back. I drove home and it was still only 6:30 p.m. I sat on my sofa and picked up my phone and stared at the text from earlier that day. Chris (name changed) wanted to do dinner.

At this point, I had gone out to dinner with a few nice men who were really good, Godly guys. Getting back on the dating horse had not been easy. I made the decision after lots of prayer to be open to men who approached me. It wasn't comfortable at the beginning after 25 years of being married, but I made myself do it and did enjoy the company. I liked Chris and he expressed a genuine interest in pursuing a very real relationship with me. As I looked at Chris's text, I decided I would text him back and spend the evening with him; it definitely would be better than sitting home alone! I wrote out the text and felt the Holy Spirit nudge me a gentle "no, not tonight". The more I thought about our conversations, the more I knew I couldn't do it. Chris was ready to dive into a full-on relationship and I knew in my heart that I didn't want the same thing with him. I just wanted to fill the void. I just didn't want to feel so lonely.

I erased the text and put my phone down.

"Okay Lord. I feel lonely tonight, but I trust you"

I began to process the flood of emotions. I knew I didn't want to be alone forever, and I liked Chris, but it wasn't fair to lead him on further. I knew he wasn't someone I wanted a serious relationship with, and I would end up hurting him if I used him in the time being just to fill a void. I bravely chose to stay home alone instead of hurting him. Finally, I decided to address this achy feeling and fear of being alone. Calling Chris that night would have evaded the feelings of loneliness for that evening, but I would have been avoiding a deeper issue of learning to be okay being by myself.

I got up and turned on some worship music, got my journal and poured out my heart to the Lord. My life had drastically changed and now I had to learn to be alone without feeling so lonely. I looked up Scriptures and wrote them down.

"Be strong and courageous. Do not be afraid or terrified because of them, for the Lord your God goes with you; He will never leave nor forsake you."
DEUTERONOMY 31:6

"Turn to me and be gracious to me; for I am lonely and afflicted".
PSALM 25:16

"So do not fear, for I am with you, do not be dismayed, for I am your God I will strengthen you and help you; I will uphold you with my righteous right hand."
PSALM 41:10

To be honest, I wanted someone with skin on them to help my lonely heart. I wanted someone in the flesh to talk to and interact with, but that night I knew that God wanted to fill the emptiness in a deeper way. I reread the Scriptures I had written down. I surrendered my loneliness to Him and asked Him to help me. After a few minutes of listening to the worship music and meditating on the Scriptures I wrote down, I began to sense the Lord's presence in such a beautiful way I realized that the ache had subsided, and that God was proud of me for bringing it to Him. Then I wrote down this phrase:

I may feel the loneliness, but I AM NEVER ALONE.

JESUS is enough.

I felt it. The feelings of loneliness were real, after all I had been married 25 years, but the TRUTH was… I was *not* alone! I made the choice to proactively deal with the loneliness. I thought of all the things I had never done alone. I had never taken a destination trip alone. I had never even gone to a movie alone! So, I made a list and concluded that I would begin to do some of them, *alone.*

I started to feel a nervous excitement. I wanted to take a trip, so I began researching a place to go and started planning. I looked up hotels and flights and budgeted it all out. I can still remember the adrenaline as I booked the flight and hotel. When I clicked the button to reserve them, my heart raced! I was moving forward, and I felt such a surge of victory!

That first trip alone, changed so much for me! I met so many amazing people and enjoyed seeing new places; and the independence and accomplishment I felt boosted my confidence to another level. It was one of the best decisions I ever made and changed my perspective incredibly! Was I nervous? Yes. Was it all easy? No. However, this brave step catapulted me to a new season where I didn't despise being alone. In fact, I found a new courageous joy in my season of doing things by myself, with myself and for myself! It was life-changing, and it will be for you too! I quickly learned that being alone did not have to be lonely. As I began to heal and step out of my comfort zones more, I found myself excited and longing for time alone. I looked forward to trips by myself, so I started traveling more and more. Each time I checked into an airport or sat at a restaurant by myself, I learned more and more about the woman I was and the Jesus I loved. My confidence began to soar, and I felt happier and more excited about my future than ever before. I could hear God clearer and each step I took seemed so sure. I was alone, but the loneliness was gone, completely. I spent the next 18 months having the time of my life and was closer and more aware of the God inside of me than I had ever experienced when I was married. I am not saying you can't have that if you are married. But without being intentional with time alone, we can lose ourselves in our titles such as wife and mom instead of getting lost in our main identity. As women, we wear so many hats and often have so many relationships that being alone for very long is not comfortable for us and it takes time alone to find who we really are outside of the "hats" we wear. I have met with many women in all walks of life in my counseling practice who felt like they have lost who they are, many are married and yet feel very lonely, single women who go from one relationship to another just to avoid being alone, or women who are launching their last child to college and find themselves feeling alone and disconnected to who they once were. So, I want to challenge you today to create time alone and see just how far you can stretch yourself and discover who you are and what you are capable of in Christ, alone.

―――――― *Rise To Brave!* ――――――

Maybe you also have struggled with loneliness. Maybe your life is so consumed with people and obligations that you rarely feel lonely, but you also rarely remember the "girl" you once were.

Sometimes, we literally must do things *afraid*. I encourage you to ask the Holy Spirit to change your mindset regarding loneliness vs. being alone. Yes, it's only normal in traumatic transitions to feel lonely at times, but God will never leave you nor forsake you. He is always with you and He wants to show up for you!

So, it's time to lean into a little more bravery today. What is something you have never done all by yourself? It might be as simple as planning a night out and going to a movie, maybe it is treating yourself to a nice dinner by yourself, or it could be taking off and going hiking for the day. Whatever it is, take the time to write down three things you have never done alone and set a goal with a timeline to do at least one of them in the next 31 days. I want you to choose events that put you on edge or seem a little scary to you. Go back and read the Scriptures above and know that God will give you the strength and will always be with you. Move forward bravely, take action and watch God flood you with new confidence and joy!

1.

2.

3.

I commit to completing my first action by _____ (date). Remember, bravery and confidence are built, one actionable step at a time! You do hard things, and the outcomes will blow your mind!

"The Lord our God said to us in Horeb, "You have stayed long enough at this mountain, Turn and take your journey and go to the hill country of the Amorites. See, I have set the land before you. Go in and take possession."

Deuteronomy 1:6-8

17

FEEL FEAR AND DO IT ANYWAY

*I*f you are in a season of grief right now, fear can really be consuming! I remember feeling paralyzed by fear as I faced my new normal of single parenting and starting over. If you have been abandoned by a spouse, lost someone you loved, or are facing a new season in life and everything is completely *not normal*, you know what I mean. Honestly, for some time, all the new things I had to learn to do on my own seemed overwhelming. Paying all the bills, recovering financially, planning for retirement by myself, talking about sex and dating, dropping kids off to college alone, hearing scary news all by yourself, hospital stays, buying cars, launching businesses with no savings, cleaning out a life of 25 years alone and leaving the home you raised your kids in…. life was daunting and each new event I faced came with a new set of fears.

Yet the more things I pushed through, the more courage I felt. As I took one brave step at a time, I began to experience surprising confidence instead of the overwhelming fear. You have to be willing to feel the fear and do it scared anyway if you want to move from where you are to where you want to be.

Fear is a natural emotion. Unfortunately, most people allow fear to stop them from taking the steps necessary to achieve their dreams and have the life God planned out for them.

Think about some of the great women in the Bible who changed the course of history: Esther-- she felt afraid and knew she may die for facing the King. Rahab also felt afraid and could have been killed for hiding the spies. Mary was terrified when given the assignment to carry a baby out of wedlock. They are women just like you and me. They felt afraid and experienced fear. But the reason we are still talking about them thousands of years later isn't because they didn't feel fear, it is because they did and decided to trust God and move forward anyway!

I used to have a real phobia of flying. I would begin experiencing anxiety at least two weeks before the trip and never flew alone because of it. So, when I divorced, I decided that I was going to book a flight and take a trip to California all by myself! I knew it would be pivotal for me to get on the plane, spend a week away all by myself and then fly back home. I knew that there was a life I dreamed of on the other side of fear and avoiding feeling it would keep me bound to a life with small walls and limits. I boarded that plane, sat down in the middle seat and blasted worship music so loud in my ear pods for the 3-hour flight that both my neighbors felt the power of the Holy Ghost! That trip was one of the most life changing and fulfilling trips of my life and doing it afraid launched me into a new level of confidence and experiences literally all around the world.

Why am I sharing this with you? Because life is full of opportunities and success waiting to be achieved for those who dare to take the risk. And the best way to overcome fear, is to take action. I cannot tell you how many times I would feel fear, and immediately correct my spirit by saying out loud, "No! I do not have a spirit of fear, I have a spirit of power, of love and of sound mind." With each new fear that I would face and chose to go at it anyway, I became more and more confident and experienced more and more of God's abundance. Most of our fears are self- created. We scare ourselves by imagining negative outcomes to the things we long to pursue.

Thankfully, we can also imagine the positive outcomes possible when we choose to take action in spite of our fears. I may have been scaring myself by imagining the plane crashing, but I decided to fill my ears and mouth with facts from the Word and chose to imagine myself laying out on the beach and hearing the crash of waves. I have used affirmations, the truth of the Word, and visualizing positive outcomes to break through all kinds of fear and push myself into action. Another tip when dealing with fear is to take something we fear and make it fun. A couple of years after my divorce, I was invited to speak at a women's conference. I was still learning the ropes of my single life and I caught myself falling back into some fearful thinking about sharing my story. So, I decided to take the anxious feelings about sharing my story in front of a large crowd and buy me something fun to wear for the event. I went and bought myself a stunning backless (gasp) black outfit with super-HOT red shoes that had me feeling like a million bucks when I stepped on that stage! Truthfully, it gave me the confidence boost I needed in that moment to feel fear and do it anyway and the event couldn't have gone better! Was it the dress? The shoes? Obviously not, but the fact that I decided to acknowledge my fear and bring some fun into the moment took away the power of my fears and gave me a new perspective to walk in!

—————————— *Rise To Brave!* ——————————

What fear is it that the enemy taunts you with? Is it fear of speaking up? Fear of doing something alone? Fear of being rejected or labeled? Fear of failing? Take some time today and ask God how you can embrace that fear and step into action. Yes, moving through fear takes intentional brave action steps and many times, it isn't easy. I applaud you for every brave step, big or small! I want to encourage you to have fun while you are walking in your healing or embracing new seasons of life! When you feel fear, acknowledge what you are scaring yourself with by imagining the worst and visualize yourself succeeding and go for it! God has so much more for us than what we are experiencing, and He wants to do something BIG with each one of our lives if we will take the step and do it even when we feel afraid!

What is one step of action you are willing to take today in spite of fear?

_____

_____

_____

"God has not given us a spirit of fear, but of power, love and of sound mind."

2 Timothy 1:7

18

EMBRACING THE "F WORD" – FORGIVING OTHERS

I stared at the screen, blinking hard to focus on the words I was about to write. It was midmorning at my office. I opened my email and began to type, *"Hello. I would like to meet you in the Starbucks parking lot in 30 minutes to talk. See you there, Kathy"*. Click. Sent.

I stood up immediately, grabbed my keys and headed out the door to meet the woman my husband had betrayed our marriage with. I knew this day would come. God and I had been talking about it for a while, and I had spent hours trying to wrap my mind around doing this and authentically meaning it. This particular day, I woke up and knew it was time. My heart was free. The blame, resentment, the hatred, the anger, it was gone. Replaced with a tenderness and grace to see her differently. She was loved by my heavenly Father and offered forgiveness from Him just like me. All the hours of tears, journaling, praying and begging God to heal my heart had brought me to this profound place. It left me speechless and peaceful where there had been no peace before. Forgiveness. The great beginning of my new life. A life without being victimized or controlled by my hurt anymore.

I pulled up my car, put it in park, and opened the door. I didn't come out immediately, I hesitated just to look around and see if she was there. My eyes met her across the parking lot. I got out of my car and walked to meet her. I remember feeling calm and relieved as I stood looking at her. It was almost like God escorted me to meet her. In fact, of course He was with me, and I felt a grace that only He could give.

"Thank you for meeting me. I have been praying about this for some time. I know about the details of your past relationship with my husband. I am moving my life forward and expect there to be no more contact with any of my family ever again. I want you to know I forgive you and have been praying for you and your husband's restoration as well." Tears began to fall from her eyes, rolling after each other like a stream. Forgiving her freed me from the emotional attachment to the pain of that past wound.

Let me tell you what forgiveness is and what it is not. Forgiveness is a process and it's about extending mercy to those who have harmed us, even if they don't "deserve" it. Forgiveness is NOT about condoning the person's behavior or implying what they did was okay. Nor is it about forgetting what happened or being a doormat to further abuse. But the benefits from letting go and forgiving is well worth the effort. Thankfully, she wasn't the supermodel I had envisioned (I had hoped she was ugly, but she wasn't) and honestly as we began to talk, I realized she was broken in many ways just as I was. I wasn't prepared for the emotion that followed... I felt no hate or disgust, and genuinely had empathy for her. Before you scream bull-crap at me or think that I'm some extra super-saint woman (because I have my flaws, believe me), let me say that it could only be God that graced me in that encounter. It was like I saw her through His eyes and not through my angry, wounded soul.

My point in telling you this is that the enemy lies. The enemy exaggerates. The enemy wants to mess your mind up and cause you to give up. He wants to keep you from your healing. He doesn't want you to be brave or courageous. He wants to keep you angry, depressed, broken and unforgiving. It's ALL lies and the fact that you are even reading this little book; and taking 31 steps to a brave new you is proof that the enemy will not win! Unforgiveness is a prison and a playground for the enemy that steals from us physically, emotionally, and spiritually. Withholding forgiveness has not only been shown to increase depression and anxiety but has been connected to physical ailments such as weakened immune systems, reduced sleep, high blood pressure and cardiovascular problems. So basically, holding onto unforgiveness keeps us sick. But be of good courage friend! Remember, forgiveness is a process and sometimes, you must choose to forgive again and again. All you must do is take one step at a time. The more steps you make, the more you will heal. Soon you will be running full speed towards the beautiful future that God has planned for you.

Rise to Brave!

1. Choose one person, situation or group of people you want to focus on forgiving. An important part of this step is to WANT to forgive them. If you don't want to forgive, you may not be ready yet, but God can give you a heart to forgive when you ask Him for it.

2. Acknowledge how these painful experiences made you feel. Forgiveness doesn't mean we ignore our feelings and dismiss our hurt. Some people experience healing through writing a letter to the person telling them everything they want to say. Let out all the anger and hatred you have felt. Don't hold back. When you have let it all out, tear the paper into small pieces or burn it as a representation of letting go of the built-up anger or resentment.

3. Ask yourself: How does holding onto this grudge, anger, resentment, or sadness help me in my life? How does holding onto these negative emotions hurt me? Then release your pain and hurt to your loving Father and let Him finish the work you just began.

"Love prospers when
a fault is forgiven but
dwelling on it separates
close friends."

Proverbs 17:9

19

PANIC ATTACK

I ran out the door of the Cheesecake Factory, tugging at my clothes, yanking off my sweater and continuing to take off my shirt. My sister ran out after me, frantically yelling, "Where are you going?" I felt like I was suffocating and desperately wanted to get my clothes off me as fast as I could. I gasped for air. My sister caught up to me, threw her arms around me, locking me in her embrace, and looked into my eyes firmly and said, "Stop! What are you doing? Kathy, YOU ARE OKAY!"

But I wasn't--I was having a panic attack.

We had been eating lunch at the Cheesecake Factory and out of nowhere I felt a constriction in my chest. It became so tight that I couldn't breathe. My first instinct was to reach for a glass of water. But as an afterthought, all I wanted was to run out of there and free myself from any clothing on my body that constricted me. I had never had a panic attack before. It felt like my soul and my body weren't congruent. I realized later that my physical body probably couldn't process the trauma and stress I was experiencing, so it was attempting to free itself from it. Stress and trauma do crazy things to your body, so learning how to respond to a panic attack was new for me.

The enemy comes in to steal, kill, and destroy. Triggers or negative thoughts do not come with a warning or an alert telling you when they will show up for you to get prepared. They just come out of nowhere, leaving you to fend for yourself at that moment. I would be in my car, sitting at a red light when my mind would just wander elsewhere, and become so foggy because it was cluttered with the weight of my world at that moment. I would just be somewhere and…. BAM! Thoughts would pour in: "You will not get through this." "Your friends won't stay around." "You will be broken financially, and you will miss out on family memories now…" The thoughts were so brutal. During these kinds of instances, the fear and anxiety would get so loud in my head and affect my body. This is when grounding yourself to the present and truth is necessary, as you must take back control of the uncontrollable situations and moments. I reached inside my purse for the 3 X 5 cards that I had made a few weeks earlier from a sheet of Scriptures that a dear friend had given me. I was determined to fight the negative emotions that often came flooding in. Remember, the truth was hard for me in moments of attack on my mind. One evening, I wrote scriptures out on cards, and I carried them with me wherever I went. I fumbled through my purse, but they weren't there. Desperately, I opened the console between the seats and there the cards were. Cars behind me honked, but I focused on trying to read one out loud, and then another. As I did that, I felt the uncontrollable anxiety lessen. I could feel life coming back into me. Those cards were everything to me during that season. God's Word on those notecards were repeatedly a love transfusion of hope. Listen, we must do our part to act our way out of grief. We must keep getting up! Sometimes, when we go through seasons where we feel lost in life, it feels like we completely cannot function, much less read a book or study on how to deal with our pain or grief! We may fight to just survive the day, much less conquer it, and that is okay if we don't stay there.

I want to encourage someone right now that if the only thing you can do is turn on worship music and lay there, then do it. If you can't even bring yourself to read a book, then just turn on an encouraging or inspirational podcast or YouTube video. Why? Because I have great news for you! Eventually faith and hope will pierce through the darkness! So, regardless of how you feel, just keep letting the positive input and truths from God's word (and other good inspiring encouragement) saturate your mind and atmosphere. Ultimately, His compassion will break through the veil of depression and hopelessness. You will find strength to take baby steps, and then tackle braver and bigger steps. You may feel nothing as you worship or have messages or exhortations playing, but the consistent effort of just hitting play will move you forward and shift your atmosphere. It takes courage and strength to keep going and not give up!

I want to share a verse that I wrote out and put on my mirror in the bathroom during one of my hardest seasons in life. This Scripture verse became a literal lifeline of hope for me. I hope it will do the same for you. Yes, your life at certain moments may suck. Yet you have EVERYTHING you need to walk through it all.

When the moment seems hard or overwhelming, remind yourself and the devil, *"I have everything I need for this life and godliness!"* It is a moment in time, a scene of life and you will get through as you take one brave action step at a time.

———————— *Rise To Brave!* ————————

Go to my website at www.kathysmalley.com and search for the Scripture Cards. I have created a template of the scriptures I carried with me and read OUT LOUD every day to activate my faith and bring truth to light. Print them out and cut along the perforation and speak them out loud every day. Be brave and resolve to "do the do". You are already here, so you might as well reach for all God has for you! Each action step is building you up and reframing your world.

Again, the science confirms Biblical principles on why speaking out loud is so important to imprint into our memory and create environment change. This step will be significant for your mindset whether you are on the mountain top or in the valley!

Also, here is a practical tip when you have a panic attack or are feeling anxious:

Look around the room/place where you are. Describe 3 things you see in detail. I know there are other methods for grounding (i.e., 5,4,3,2,1); however, I found that focusing and describing 3 things worked very well for me and other clients in my therapy practice.

Describe 3 things you see right now as practice:

_____

_____

_____

Pick one of the Scriptures from my website or choose your own and write it below:

_____

_____

_____

_____

_____

_____

"God's divine power has given us everything we need for life and for godliness. This power was given to us through knowledge of the one who called us by His own glory and integrity."

2 Peter 1:3 GWT

26

IDENTITY IN CHRIST

"If there is no enemy within you,
then the enemy can do you no harm."

I did not understand the meaning of that phrase until April 4, 2013, when my relationship of 25 years dissolved before my eyes after I caught my husband in an affair. My heart fell into my stomach and all I had believed and the identity of who I was shattered into a tiny million pieces. The anger, betrayal and lost love left me hurting in a way I had never experienced. Although my husband was indeed abandoning me, in time I would realize that his abandonment was God's protection for my life and destiny. The process of being whole would take vast amounts of courage. I came to realize that the pain from that trauma was not to throw me off course, but an opportunity to learn how deeply and powerfully I could put my trust in God who is always faithful. I came to understand how God could take my pain and establish the truth of my identity in a world of lost souls.

If you don't make it your business to understand who you are and what you are capable of, the world or religion will enroll you in their limited philosophy. The world loves to "hashtag" our life with things like #divorced #abused or #unworthy. I realized I didn't want to be hash-tagged for my future. I had a foundation and relationship with Jesus Christ as Lord and Savior, but the trauma I went through forced me to find a deeper identity and intimacy with Christ. The best decision I ever made was to do the inner work to let go of the pain of the past and focus on moving forward into the future, stronger and braver in my identity in Him.

God can do an incredible work with women who will own their wounds. Truly realizing *Whose I am* and authentically *who I am*, required me to pursue a certainty and conviction about my identity. This only came as I established myself in the truth of God's Word concerning my identity. God has put His identity on/in us through Jesus Christ.

Romans 8:15-18 TPT says it so beautifully,

And you did not receive the spirit of religious duty, leading you back into the fear of never being good enough. But you have received the Spirit of full acceptance, enfolding you into the family of God. And you will never feel orphaned, for as He rises up within us, our spirits join Him in saying the words of tender affection, "Beloved Father!" For the Holy Spirit makes God's fatherhood real to us as He whispers into our innermost being, "You are God's beloved child!"

Oh how I love God's Word! We have received FULL ACCEPTANCE! Though I had been incredibly rejected in my relationship with my husband, I could re-establish my identity through Jesus that I was indeed not rejected, but FULLY ACCEPTED! That makes me want to shout even as I'm writing this! When we can truly grasp what God has promised in this verse with certainty and conviction, then we will not be moved by other's opinions, nor our own fears! Our trials and traumas do not define us! There is only One (the Lord God Almighty) that defines us and He gave His son Jesus, who died on a cross, rose again and is seated in Heaven making intercession for us (John 17:22)! God sent the Holy Spirit to help us on this earth until we see Jesus face to face (John 14:26). This is glorious news! It does not matter what you have gone through or even what you may have done, God's love and His promises are so grand that He has already made a way for you to bravely move forward victoriously! He came to give us a life full of abundance. The situation or painful place that you are in was not a surprise to God. God knows the end from the beginning and has already paid for your victory through the finished work of the cross! Take heart courageous woman, you can move from apathy and uncertainty to absolute confidence of identity that will move you to a place of influence and impact. I promise you the work and the surrender will be worth it. You are God's beloved child—never forget that.

Rise to Brave!

What "hashtags" are you letting define you? Maybe you are fearing being labeled by others, or maybe you are labeling yourself. Write 5 hashtags that you don't want to define your life:

#

#

#

#

#

Now write 5 hashtags that are your TRUE identity:

#

#

#

#

#

Example: #unwanted vs. #soughtafter #unworthy vs. #cherished #broke vs. #abundant

"He whispers into our inner most being, 'you are God's beloved child.'"

Romans 8:16b TPT

21

SETTING BOUNDARIES

I pushed the door open trying to escape the office. I could feel the surge of emotions rising as tears blinded my eyes. I could see the building exit sign as I hurriedly turned the corner in the long and lonely hallway. I was desperate to get outside as the tears poured--blurring my vision and clouding my contacts. My knees buckled beneath me as I stepped onto the last step and the weight of my body forced me to sit down as I sobbed uncontrollably.

I had signed the papers that would begin the process to end my 25-year marriage. The decision to file for divorce was excruciatingly painful and months of prayer, sleepless nights and wrestling with fear, shame, and my faith preceded that pivotal moment. As I'm writing this, I can close my eyes and see that woman sitting on the bottom step and I want to wrap my arms around her and tell her how brave she was.

Staying was hard, but leaving took a form of grit and courage that I never knew I had. As a woman who loves Jesus, His Word and the beautiful covenant of Godly marriage, I am not condoning, encouraging, or discouraging divorce. As a therapist, I have watched men and women give up far too easily and yet others stay far too long in horrible abuse. Leaving the toxic relationship that resulted from my husband's addictions and abuse wasn't about a lack of faith or belief. I fought religious narratives that echoed loudly from my past accusing me that "all divorce was a sin"; but it was about an act of love and bravery. Letting go and deciding to no longer stay in my marriage was the hardest (and oddly) the most loving boundary I had ever drawn. It was hard for all the reasons you can imagine (and all the ones you can't begin to know unless you have been there) and yet I felt love towards my husband, myself, and our children.

After years of broken boundaries, filing for divorce was actually the bravest decision to hold to my boundaries of honesty, trust and faithful covenant. Even though I was a licensed therapist and had lots of book knowledge and training about boundaries, codependency, and enabling behaviors, there were many steps taken before I followed through and drew the line in the sand with the man that I had loved for so long. Setting boundaries in abusive relationships can trigger fear of abandonment, rejection, financial loss, physical harm, shame and so much more. If you are in a relationship tainted with abuse or addiction, I am here right now to tell you, I know how hard and how scary it is, but you can leave. You need to leave. The destruction of staying in an unhealthy situation can be so much more detrimental in the long run.

Maybe you're not in an abusive relationship, but in a relationship that drains you emotionally, or isn't healthy for you. Maybe it is a relationship that doesn't support your core values or beliefs and leaves you feeling guilty or angry. It could be a child who continues to forget school items and you continue to rescue them by bringing the items to them. It takes lots of courage to set boundaries around your relationships. It isn't easy and often requires us to face hard realities about ourselves, our childhood or even our parents. I have spoken to thousands of women who believe they have no choice over certain relationships and allow others to take advantage of them or pull energy from them emotionally; and many times, it is family relationships that are emotionally or verbally toxic.

Boundaries are powerful tools for you and the people you love to be drawn closer together, rather than further apart. They can create a space that allows us to protect our personal values. Boundaries can also allow us to conserve our emotional energy. Setting boundaries can keep us from trying to rescue others and carry things God never intended for us to carry (which could cause us to become resentful or bitter).

Maybe you need to set boundaries around your time, commitments or your social media. Jesus and the Bible lay out clear examples of how to live in healthy boundaries. Jesus ate healthy foods, he got sleep when He needed and even took naps (yay!). He took time to relax, and at times, withdrew from others to be alone. He sought company with friends, and He didn't give into His own mother when she tried to pull Him away from a crowd He was ministering to!

These are all examples of healthy boundaries. We can set loving boundaries without blame, attacking others, or betraying ourselves through healthy communication and listening to the Holy Spirit.

Rise To Brave!

It's time to take ownership of what is yours and let go of what's not. When we practice boundaries, we take ownership of four things: our thoughts, our feelings, our bodies, and our decisions. Likewise, we let other people take ownership of theirs rather than taking responsibility for what isn't really yours.

When it comes to toxic relationships, the first thing you want to do is to pray about it and thank God for giving you wisdom. Prayer is power! Are you enabling their behavior by staying in the relationship or do you believe setting boundaries is judgmental, unloving, or unkind? If you answered yes to any of these, then it is time to make a change. If you are in a relationship that is harmful emotionally, physically, or verbally, I encourage you to seek counsel knowing that God cares more about the individual than the institution of marriage or the status of the relationship. Make the decision to bravely exercise your right to healthy boundaries. Most of us know when we are being taken advantage of or when our personal space or needs are being dismissed as unimportant.

If you are not sure what limit/limits you need to set in your relationships, start with these questions to consider:

- Is someone blaming me for something that is their responsibility?
- What is reasonable for someone to ask of me, and what is not?
- Am I taking on responsibilities that are not my own or am I feeling resentful or frustrated with a relationship?
- What are my expectations from this person? Are those reasonable?

• What do I need to communicate so that my boundaries/limits are understood?

Give yourself permission to have needs, limits, and boundaries. You are allowed to say no. You are allowed to ask for what you want or need. Your thoughts and feelings matter. You are valuable and most importantly, you are God's precious daughter – treasured beyond measure!

As you went through the questions, what is one situation and with whom do you need to set a new boundary that will honor yourself and them?

_____

_____

_____

What boundary needs to be upheld that you have allowed to be broken?

_____

_____

_____

Make a commitment to implement a needed boundary in one of your relationships this week.

As you finish today, meditate on this Scripture. I know it is most likely referencing literal boundaries but ask the Holy Spirit to show you where not drawing boundaries has caused loss and hardship in your own life. Ask the Holy Spirit to give you wisdom and courage as you establish boundaries in your life.

"There are those who move boundary stones; they pasture flocks they have stolen."

Job 24:2

22

HARD CONVERSATIONS

"When we avoid difficult conversations, we trade short term discomfort for long term dysfunction"
~ PETER BROMBERG.

*W*e've previously talked about facing reality and one of the best ways we can accomplish that is by *doing the hard things*. You may think that you don't like to do hard things. And I get that. There were days that just getting my kids to school felt overwhelming and going to the gym seemed completely out of the question. But little by little and brave step by brave step, you can and WILL do the hard things.

One of those hard things is deciding to stop avoiding the hard conversations.

Most people really don't like confrontation, and will do anything to avoid it, but what if I told you that the best relationships are ones often created on the other side of hard conversations? When I was faced with my husband's addiction to prescription painkillers; it required deciding to have hard conversations that were uncomfortable or choosing to live in continued dysfunction.

As I inched forward toward my healing, I knew I had to do the hard things and learn how to embrace hard conversations instead of avoiding them. This became a pivotal place of growth in my relationships with my kids, my family, friendships, and business partners. Most of the conversations I needed to have were often avoided because of something I *imagined* would happen. I created false narratives in my mind about how the person would respond or what would happen instead of looking at it as an opportunity for long-term benefits.

After the revelation of my husband's affair, I shared with you that I faced "the other woman" (See "Embracing the F Word-Forgiveness" previously). That conversation created clear boundaries and empowered me to know the truth instead of believing lies. Every one of us has probably avoided having conversations. As a single mom of two boys, I faced many awkward conversations about girls, pornography, and even masturbation! Did I want to talk to my boys about those things? No. Did they want me to talk to them about those things? Double heck no! But I can tell you that having those conversations created space for having a lot of other conversations throughout their life that have led to me having incredible relationships with both my son's into adulthood.

Confronting and having hard conversations with the "other women" and my boys were example of steps of bravery. Was it easy? No, but the strength that flowed from that encounter built a courage that continues to grow in every area of my life. Deciding to take the step to have hard conversations will build your bravery as well!

Today may be a little harder but push through and watch God work on your behalf! What is one hard conversation that you need to have? Write it below.

_____

_____

_____

_____

_____

_____

_____

My greatest fear is _____.

I fear_____ by

imagining_____

Now, ask the Holy Spirit to check your motives behind that hard conversation. Once you feel peace from the Lord, determine how and when you will have it.

Once you do it, sign and date below and note any insights that God showed you through your conversation.

_____   _____

Name   Date

"Do not be afraid of them; the Lord your God Himself will fight for you."

Deuteronomy 3:22

23

BE CLEAR WHY YOU ARE HERE

I have a beautiful friend who I met through social media in the middle of my mess when I was launching a new business and overcoming my self-limiting beliefs. She vulnerably shared a personal story that gave her clarity why she was here and what she wanted to be for herself and those she loved. What she authentically shared left an imprint on me and I hope it does for you as well....

It was a frigid February in Fargo, North Dakota...

I was in the middle of my junior year in college as a biology major and running track on an athletic scholarship. I knew my parents couldn't afford to pay for college, so I found myself setting a standard of achievement for my siblings, so they too could go to college on scholarships.

Growing up in a rural community came with many blessings. I grew up with a strong work ethic, surrounded by family (my grandparents, aunts and uncles were all on the same farm) and taught the value of sound character and core values.

From a young age, I was exceptionally curious. Rarely did I feel like I fit in and would often find myself day-dreaming while running the country roads. I realized that I saw a different vision for my life, but I had yet to find that example in any woman around me. I quickly noticed that as a woman in a rural community, you can't shine too bright, dream too big or speak too loudly or ruffle anyone else's feathers. I heard gossip, limiting narratives, and religious shaping about who a woman "should" be daily. However, something in me KNEW I was made for more and I felt connected to my Creator, listening to the whispers to "keep being authentically me."

I rooted my worth in achievement, as it was my way of getting the love I craved from my Dad. Growing up on a farm prepped my entrepreneurial spirit for uncertainty. We didn't know what the crop yield would be each season. It gave me the understanding that patient persistence is necessary in life, and that you can't sow and reap in the same season. And it taught me that our beliefs are hard-wired and shaped by our environment at a young age. Growing up in a double - wide trailer, I watched my mom raise four kids and do it like a champion, but I struggled to see myself in her story.

What I wasn't prepared for were the results of my first pregnancy test in February 2003. I had been accepted to graduate school at Northwestern Health Sciences University just a month before to get my Doctorate in Chiropractic. It elated me to share with my family that I would make the big move to Minneapolis after I completed my undergraduate degree. So, when I saw the + sign on the test, I dropped to my knees in anxiety, completely overwhelmed at just 20 years old. I was shaking, crying and imagining the disappointment in my parents' and grandparents' eyes.

Although I decided I would keep this baby, I had no idea that experience would shape the next decade of my life. When I went home to tell my family; I was met with what I expected – their disappointment, fear, shame and embarrassment. I knew that I would not "make this right", until I was married or stayed home to raise my baby like a woman should. I internalized this shame, knowing I was not ready for marriage and still desired to attend graduate school. I pushed every emotion as far down as I could and decided to move. I would start my first trimester in my doctorate program with a 3-month-old and work for my worth for the next decade of my life, never letting vulnerability, fear, or my true self be seen. I was going to PROVE my worth to everyone - including myself, by validating it with success.

I wouldn't have this self-awareness, until a decade later as I hit rock bottom. This realization came after a cycle of abusive relationships (both personally and professionally), failed businesses, a void so big in the pit of my stomach and a heart that I tried to fill with everything, but self-worth and self-love. I had another little girl, and now, I was a single mom with two daughters from two different dads. I carried more shame and guilt than I can express in words. It was in that pivotal moment that I fell to my knees on my bathroom floor, praying for someone or something to come into my life to show me WHO I was supposed to be and what my purpose was on this earth. I made a promise to God, "I will be your most humble servant," if He would just show me the way. He told me to look in the mirror, radically forgive myself and start new. And I have kept that promise every day since.

My friend achieved her doctorate, started multiple businesses as a single mom, and has risen as an impact-driven leader in her industry all because she allowed God to identify her worth and value outside of accomplishments and gave clarity on who she desired to be.

Every woman deserves to experience authenticity and abundance. As women, we often put on the faces of who we think we need to be just to feel accepted. Very few vulnerably reveal their story and do the work necessary to shed the layers and find the core of who we truly are! My hope is that you know you were put on this earth on purpose, for a purpose! God has a path planned for you and NOW is your time to walk it. Bravely face your limiting beliefs and take the necessary action to transform your life.

— *Rise To Brave!* —

Of the thousands of women that I have worked with, very few have been able to answer this question immediately: What do you want? If we don't know what we want, our days are as productive and intentional as getting into our cars without a GPS. We set our destination for "point unknown" and the results are a direct reflection of our uncertainty. Clarity gives us certainty and certainty breeds confidence. We know what to do when we can see where we are going and have an action plan to get there.

So today, it's time to get clear about your purpose. Grab a piece of paper and write out a short vision/purpose/mission statement. What do you believe? What do you love to do?

What are you good at? This statement will likely stem from the most challenging parts of your story. What moves you? What makes you feel the most fulfilled or lights you up inside? What kind of future do you long for? What kind of impact would you like to create? When we are living in alignment with the purpose of our life, it will automatically serve and benefit those around us as well.

"I urge you to live a life worthy of the calling you have received."

Ephesians 4:1(b)

24

CHANGE YOUR FOOD, CHANGE YOUR MOOD

*T*rauma takes a toll on your physical health and, at the same time, affects your mental health. Some people's response to stress is indulging in food, while for some, eating won't even be an option. As I went through my tumultuous season of trauma, I reacted physically to the stress in my body; I had hair loss, broke out in hives, headaches and other physical ailments. Anyone who has experienced grief or trauma can attest to the cost of being in a state of stress for an extended period. Trauma can trigger the "fight or flight" response which releases hormones.

During the fight or flight response your body is trying to prioritize and anything it doesn't need for immediate survival is placed on the back burner. This means that digestion, reproductive and growth hormone production and tissue repair can all be temporarily halted. Our fight or flight response was designed to help us survive but living in a prolonged state of high alert and stress can be detrimental to your physical and mental health.

Your autonomic nervous system is a delicate balancing act between your sympathetic nervous system and your parasympathetic nervous system. Both networks involuntarily react to the surrounding environment. Your sympathetic nervous system handles how your body reacts to danger and is responsible for the fight or flight response. Your parasympathetic nervous system is responsible for maintaining homeostasis, which is your body's built-in stability monitor (think of it like a generator—making sure everything from your body temperature to your water intake is functioning smoothly). It makes sure things are balanced. It works to relax you, conserve and restore energy in your body. As a human, you need both the sympathetic and parasympathetic systems to run properly.

During extended periods of stress, your sympathetic and parasympathetic nervous systems can become imbalanced. That's why it is so very important to bravely face the steps you need to take care of your body in this season. As I experienced physical indicators of chronic stress, I knew I needed to do my part physically and emotionally to abate further damage to my body. One thing we often turn to for consolation while in stress is sugar. Yep, I went there. Granted, the occasional donut or cookie is not the problem. I'm not trying to be a hard nose on this topic, but sugar is one of the major culprits that can create feelings that mimic depression and anxiety and also leave you feeling more fatigued, tired and irritated. Sugar also weakens the immune system. When I realized this, I chose to cut processed sugar out of my diet (having a body full of hives will motivate you). I cut out sugary breakfasts completely and added in mood boosting foods with good fats instead or a healthy shake. The first thing you put in your body in the morning is so important. The American diet is one of the very few diets that begins the day with caffeine and mostly sugar based options including all the breads that break down to glucose. I also realized that many fruits like cherries, bananas and grapes have a high sugar content. You can use fruit to replace the sugar; grab a cup of raspberries, strawberries, blackberries or a slice of watermelon. I also cut out sodas and increased my water intake drastically. Just increasing your water intake and cutting back on refined sugar can drastically improve brain fog and energy, as well as decrease anxious feelings or low mood. I have worked with several women who changed the foods they consumed and could get off of medications previously taken to stabilize their mood.

Another way we feed our bodies the wrong things during stress is by not eating dense foods that have protein or good carbohydrates. Carbohydrates increase levels of serotonin, a hormone that boosts mood and reduces stress. If you are having a hard time making yourself eat, drink a high protein shake that will fill in the gaps until you can get your appetite back.

I understand how hard it is to do anything when it feels like a freight train has hit your life, but courageously choosing to feed your body the right things will have a definite impact on freeing your mind in your healing journey. If you feel overwhelmed during this season and can't seem to get started on feeding your body the right way, be encouraged and ask the Holy Spirit to lead you and help you take one brave step. It will be worth it! Too many times, changing our diet seems daunting, so we quit before we even start. I want you to hear me again today: Don't despise small beginnings. That is how

I started and today I am completely free from brain fog, low energy, and any depressive or anxious feeling! Once you begin to feed your body with what it needs, you will begin to crave the right things. Start with putting in good food and the Holy Spirit will gently lead you to cut out the things that are detrimental. Take one step and be consistent, the Lord will meet you right at your point of need.

Rise To Brave

Today, I want to encourage you to start how I did. Increase your water intake and cut back on the amount of sugar you take in. Make it fun and easier by ordering a large gallon water container so you can watch your progress throughout the day. Secondly, call a friend. Tell them what you are doing and ask them to join you. You will notice a change in your brain fog and energy within a very short time as you stay consistent at it. Warning: Be prepared to pee a lot! I was stopping all the time on days I was out and about, but I promise, it changed my life as I began the journey to feed my body mood boosting foods and it all started with simply increasing my water and cutting out unnecessary sugars. Below is a list of a few extra suggestions. Look and decide to commit to implementing at least one step today. Write what you are choosing to do below and who you will ask to join you! If you are a social media person, share your new journey on your story and tag me @kathydsmalley. Let's all begin to take control over our mood and bodies as we rise up together to learn how!

1. Increase water intake. I like to wake up and have a glass of water first thing. (Average intake for women is about 11.5 cups (2.7 liters) of fluids a day for women per mayoclinic. org or you can start with half your body weight in ounces)

2. Cut out refined sugars. The first couple of days you may get a headache or seem tired. Keep going and drink lots of water.

3. Drink caffeine free and sugar free herbal teas that promote feelings of warmth and calmness. You may include this in your daily water intake.

4. Indulge moderately in some good dark chocolate.

5. Eat healthy, unrefined carbohydrates

6. Eat Avocados. They offer stress-busting Omega-3 fatty acids.

7. Do you like fish? Eat it to boost your heart health while fending off stress.

8. Snack on nuts. Nuts are a good stress buster and high in healthy fats & magnesium which has been linked to better anxiety management. (Pistachios are a great choice.)

9. Eat some citrus fruits and strawberries. They contain vitamin C which helps fight stress.

10. Add some fiber to your diet to combat stress and balance your blood sugar. Add beans, lots of greens, broccoli, kale, almonds etc. to your intake.

"It will be healing to your flesh and refreshment to your bones."

Proverbs 3:8

25

HE IS YOUR SAFE PLACE

I sat feeling anxious as the bombardment of "what ifs" flooded my mind.

"What if my daughter needed treatment physically or emotionally that I could not financially provide as a single mom?"

"What if I got terminally ill? Who would care for me? Would I be a burden on my kids?"

"What if I never have love again? What if I end up alone for the rest of my life?"

You get the picture. I had weathered the initial trauma of divorce and now I was struggling through the secondary losses. As a therapist, I had witnessed person after person come through the shock and painful agony of their initial trauma only to face the secondary losses. Now, I was personally living the same reality.

When you look around, there are always others walking through horrible situations that are even more difficult than your own. Yet pain is pain, and yes I was getting stronger but the secondary losses were tormenting me and this form of fear was snowballing in my brain. I even felt lame for feeling this way when others were going through things so much worse than I was. In this season, it was this tangled web of emotions that led me to the life-altering revelation that continues to transform me to this day.

What would I do when the questions of "what ifs" assaulted my peace? I realized I had to get honest and vulnerable with the Lord. I had to "go there" in my fears until I found the real place of surrender (not lack of belief) to the realness that God truly is trustworthy at a level most often feared. I had to fall into the arms of Jesus as my identity and all that I knew as "normal" was stripped away. It was a crossroad in my healing that changed how I processed everything.

I was determined to be strong, but I needed to accept that I didn't have to be strong with my Savior. I needed to feel it (all the emotions) and process it, not negate my feelings or fears because someone else's pain was worse. I heard the Lord whisper sweetly to me, "Tell me the very worst you fear, share your anger, it's safe to tell Me–it doesn't mean you don't trust Me."

As I laid it all out with the One who loved me most, I knew God cared about my pain and healing and every single secondary loss. God wasn't forcing me to "measure" my pain with anyone else's and asking me to just get over it. I could come to a deeper dependence and trust that would lead me to the sweetest intimacy I had ever known.

In those raw conversations with Him, I gave my "what ifs" and He would say, "then what". I gave myself permission to go there–to the worst possible scenario or outcome and walk it through with Him.

"What if my daughter needed rehab and I didn't have the money?" "Then what…" He would gently say.

"What if I have to ask others for financial help?" "Then what…" He would say.

"What if it is terribly embarrassing? What if they say no?"

With each question of Him asking "then what", God allowed me to spill every fear without the guilt of "not believing enough". I could truly cast every care on Him because He cared for me! These vulnerable, honest, and sometimes gut-wrenching conversations led me to a place of hope and peace that I wouldn't trade for anything. I found as I exposed every fear and pain to Him, I received more belief in Him as a loving Father who is completely trustworthy with everything I held most dear. It was (and still is) this intimacy, transparent and real, that grew my genuine trust and confidence in the Lord in a way like never before. He was, is and always will be my safe place.

----------------- *Rise To Brave!* -----------------

What is one thought or circumstance you are dealing with today? It can be big or small, it can even be a subconscious thought that keeps popping up. Take it to Jesus and let Him walk you through to a place of faith and hope.

1. I'm fighting to trust God with:

And then what?

2. What is behind the fear?

_____

_____

_____

And then what?

_____

_____

_____

3. What is the worst case scenario in this particular scenario?

_____

_____

_____

And then what?

_____

_____

_____

As you go to God with authenticity and vulnerability, He will gently meet you with no condemnation and complete trustworthiness. In this space of intimacy with Him, God will sweetly build your trust. Cast all your cares on Him...He is your safe place.

"Cast all your cares on Him for He cares for you".

1 Peter 5:7

26

GIVING HIM OUR YESTERDAYS AND TOMORROWS

I sat on a beautiful sofa at my dear friend's daughter's wedding shower as I looked around the beautifully decorated room. I watched as lifetime friends were chatting and laughing and telling stories of when all our kids were little. I smiled at the joy and excitement beaming from my friend's face as she celebrated her daughter's upcoming wedding to the man of her dreams. It was such a blessing to be a part of this happiness and I was thrilled to be there for such a monumental occasion! After the shower, I texted my friend and expressed how beautiful the day was and how genuinely happy I was for her and her husband to be present for this moment in their lovely daughter's life!

Moments after I sent the text, I felt an unexpected deep sadness hit me as I was driving. I thought about my four adult children, "These occasions will be different for me." The thought raced through my mind and landed in my heart. I began to contemplate my own daughters' showers, "Who would come to my children's big life occasions now?" It was true that through my traumatic divorce, I had lost many close friends that had done life with our family of six.

Now as a family of five, life and relationships had been forever affected. It wasn't that people were unkind or didn't care, it was just a part of the fall-out and life change that happened. As I stared at the road in front of me, I allowed myself to really feel the loss of not sharing my children's monumental milestones with the one who we all had loved together, their dad. No one else had experienced their first steps, no one else had gone through the broken arms or would remember watching them sleep. A tear trickled down my face and I asked the Lord, "How do I process this? How do I fill that empty spot of the memories of yesterday and the talked about tomorrows that had only been recorded by the two of us? How can I feel grief and joy at the same time? The Holy Spirit ever so gently comforted me as the words of an old hymn chorus resonated in my spirit…

One day at a time, Sweet Jesus
That's all I'm asking of You
Just give me the strength
To do every day what I have to do
Yesterday's gone sweet Jesus
And tomorrow may never be mine
Lord help me today, show me the way
One day at a time.

I decided to let the moment be just a moment. Jesus was right there with me. He knew the pain in my heart. He understood the ache of my loss and He cared completely. In His faithfulness, He would never leave me comfortless! I acknowledged the thoughts and sadness, and expressed my desire to once again give Him my yesterdays and my tomorrows. Sometimes, when we experience a trauma, tragedy, or a hard crossroads in life, we must fight not to fixate on what was (yesterday) or fear/fret about the future (tomorrow). Especially when life has been flipped upside down, we must endeavor to truly live one day at a time, and sometimes, literally one hour, or even one minute at a time! Remember, the present is the only time that matters. The future only exists in our imagination - which isn't real. The past only exists in our memories - which can be tainted with inaccuracies. When we get stuck in thinking of what was or longing to go back to the comforts of before, we miss living the present moments. We can also bring on unnecessary anxious emotions when we think of future events that don't even exist yet. You must shift your focus to be mindful of the present. This is the secret to moving out of our past patterns or emotions stuck in our subconscious and learning to live in a place of mindful present consciousness. It is healthy to acknowledge your feelings and give yourself grace for when they pop up, like I did that day leaving the beautiful shower. It is important though to stay with the present moment and not spend lengthy time creating assumptions about future events. We imagine things that have never occurred and worry about things we may likely never experience. When you live consciously, you don't react to situations, you respond. Instead of letting your emotions control your actions, you must choose to stay in the current moment without letting our subconscious thoughts that are usually formed through past experiences or our fear of a future moment rule our responses. Thankfully, we can take heart in hard moments that He is right there! He will never leave us nor forsake us and He will tenderly take our hand and walk us through every tear and heartache. It's true that living in the present is literally a "present" …a gift! He promises to give us grace for the day, so we can rest assured that when "tomorrow" becomes today and we have need, He will be all that we need.

Rise To Brave!

Maybe you can relate to the story above. Maybe certain situations remind you of what you have lost or bring a fear or dread about the future. Take a few moments today and locate yourself on the line below. Where are most of your thoughts? Mark on X on the line below. Self-awareness is a superpower for change. Discovering and acknowledging things about ourselves creates opportunities for us to pivot. When triggers come up from our past or fears about the future, decide to stay present in the current moment by acknowledging your emotions without accepting your initial thoughts as facts. Remember each day is another chance to grow and courageously press into the best version of yourself if you will be honest and stay within each present moment. Many of our relationship issues are focusing on unmet needs of the past that swing us into negative thinking and fear about the future.

It is absolutely normal to grieve the loss and process the emotions but allow Him to meet you in every moment. Begin each day by asking God for the grace (His abiding presence & strength) for THIS day. THIS is the day we have! Day by day, hour by hour, and yes sometimes, even minute by minute He will empower us to live! Take a minute and picture yourself climbing into His lap, letting Him love the pain of yesterday away and bring peace to any anxieties about tomorrow. Take a few minutes and thank Him for being ever-present with you right now, right where you are and commit to consciously being intentional with the current moments in your life.

Past   Present   Future

_____

"Refuse to worry about tomorrow, but deal with each challenge that comes your way, one day at a time. Tomorrow will take care of itself."

Matthew 6:34 TPT

27

RAISE YOUR STANDARD

I love my family beyond measure. I am so thankful for my parents who raised me to love Jesus and taught me about hard work and integrity. As I moved forward in my healing, I realized that although there were many family traits I was grateful for, there were also some family ingrained patterns I didn't want to continue repeating in my life. In my early adult years, I recognized a pattern of criticalness infiltrating my own life. I decided to break that pattern and establish a "glass half full" perspective into my thinking and actions. It wasn't easy because I had not grown up in a culture of expecting the best and being positive in adverse situations. Healing from the trauma later in my life further exposed deeper roots and thought patterns from that family pattern in my life. I did the work to "lay the ax to the root" (Matthew 3:10) of that negative pattern and raise my standards for myself. One of Tony Robbins quotes spoke to me during that time,

"If you don't set a baseline standard for what you'll accept in life, you'll find it's easy to slip into behaviors and attitudes or a quality of life that's far below what you deserve."

Attempting to change those generational propensities (spiritually a generational curse) caused me to reflect on raising my standards. I realized just how easy it would be during my trauma healing to slip back into old patterns and become apathetic towards different aspects of my life. I made a list of things that were non-negotiable. The word *non-negotiable* means:

Not open to discussion or reconsideration.

I knew that loneliness, fear, and anxiety could cause me to slip back into an attitude or behavior that would be far below what I deserved. God was doing a profound work to re-establish my identity and I needed to do my part and not settle for less than what HE said I deserved.

Of course, dating was a big one for me. I chose early in my healing to allow God to fully restore my life where I was happy and content being alone. I also asked the Lord to allow me to provide for my children and set them up financially for the future before God brought a man into my life. This was really raising the financial bar high since I had filed a bankruptcy and was starting new businesses from scratch.

Being single after 25 years of marriage (and deeply wounded) made me vulnerable in the dating scene. It felt good to be affirmed and complemented and of course physical touch was craved. I had to establish a set baseline in that area before I found myself in a tempting situation. I made a list of nonnegotiables for the men I would spend my time with and how I would spend my time with them.

During my journey, when depressive symptoms and anxiety resulted in my hair falling out and my skin breaking out in hives, I had to raise my standards with my body. This included cutting out refined sugar, consistently drinking protein and eating good carbs, and deciding to move my body every day (some days that was turning the music up loud and dancing around the house) to shift my mood and heal my emotions.

As I gained momentum in bravely moving forward towards wholeness, another non-negotiable was a daily commitment to listing a few things I was grateful for and reading scripture. These were simple things, but I made them non-negotiables. I put a stake in the ground that they were "not open for discussion or reconsideration." This helped me not to shrink back or become apathetic during exhaustion or times of depression. They were small brave markers that kept me from going two steps forward and one step back! They were an anchor that helped me maintain my standards and not be easily distracted or caught off guard when I didn't "feel like it". I had already established the standards. My "shoulds" became "musts". Was it easy? No. Did I sometimes fall short? Of course. Yet I believe God honored me for setting a higher standard.

One of the most beautiful examples of that is my husband. I set my standards high as I started to date again. My non-negotiables were specific and by setting them before I began dating, it made it easy to not be too far into a relationship before wondering how I got there. I'm human (and a very affectionate one) who thoroughly enjoys people and one-on-one time. I craved intimacy and connection, and it was hard to keep my eye on the outcome, not the moment. I did this by having standards established. The outcome of those non-negotiables was God sending me the most loving, Godly man I've ever known! He loves and serves God relentlessly and cherishes me beyond comprehension. My marriage, my relationship with Jesus, my physical body, and my emotional health are all such a redemptive fulfillment of the Scripture in Ephesians 3:20:

"Now to Him who is able to do exceedingly abundantly above all that we ask or think, according to the power that works in us, to Him be glory in the church by Christ Jesus to all generations former and ever."

I'm so thankful that the Holy Spirit led me to make non-negotiables in my life and raise my standards. We must stop limiting God! He is so for us! I believe God honored me in exceedingly beautiful ways above and beyond what I desired. Don't settle for less than what God says you deserve!

Rise To Brave!

God will give you everything you need to raise your standards and set non-negotiables in your life. Spend time asking God what non-negotiables you need to establish to raise your standards. What "shoulds" need to become "musts" for you to live a life more fulfilled? What are your nonnegotiables around your time with God, your finances, your health, your relationships, your eating habits, your self care,etc?

Remember He will empower you through the guidance and power of the Holy Spirit to help you bravely walk them out. List them below and thank God for your victory ahead of time.

_____

_____

_____

_____

_____

"Everything we could ever need for life and godliness has already been deposited in us by His divine power. For this was lavished upon us through the rich experience of knowing Hi who has called us by name and invited us to come to Him through a glorious manifestation of His goodness."

2 Peter 1:3

28

TELL SOMEONE

We were kind of a "Leave it to Beaver" family. I may be dating my age by using that phrase, but we were a nice family that lived in a nice house, in a nice neighborhood with good jobs, four kids, and four dogs. My kids attended a private Christian school, and we were involved members at a phenomenal Christian church. So, by most people's perceptions, we were truly a great family. And to be honest, we were! We had a good life. We lived life to the fullest and loved our family and others. Unfortunately, under the surface there were cracks and fissures of addictions and lies that resulted in a lot of pain and ultimately needed lots of healing.

I remember sitting at my son's basketball game after our world exploded and wondering if my current situation was written across my forehead. It sure felt like it. The rejecting thoughts were constant. "I wonder if they know." "Did my kids tell their friends? And did they tell their moms?" Or "Here I am, showing up by myself again. I bet they are wondering what I did. Do they think it was my fault?" It was so uncomfortable. In fact, it went on like that for weeks. I would go to the games, smile and make small talk while inside I was in a state of turmoil about others knowing the real truth and asking about it.

Finally, whether it was that I was just so broken and hurting or just desperate and angry enough, I decided I had to tell someone. I remember thinking about how and when or even who I would divulge such awful information. It was hard for me to stomach the truth and I certainly didn't want people looking at me with pity. Yet it got to where I knew I just couldn't keep living this way and carrying this much weight on my own in the natural realm. I knew God was with me and I somehow just kept walking, probably only because my kids needed me to be strong. I finally realized that I just had to share the burden with my closest friends.

I called four girlfriends that had known me and our family since we married. We did life together and I knew I could trust them to pray and keep my confidence. I asked them to meet me for dinner at a Mexican restaurant, of course, because there is nothing like chips and salsa and a good margarita when you must bare your soul. It was hard. It was uncomfortable. It was painful. Yet, there was something so freeing when I took that HUGE step of bravery and told someone my truth. The weight was still heavy, but it seemed just a little lighter. I guess the pain was enough that it didn't matter if they judged me, or pitied me, or didn't believe me. I wasn't telling them for anyone, but myself. I needed to speak the truth and bring it to light and have someone else carry some of it with me. It was truly one of the hardest things I had ever done. No one wants to be looked down on or rejected or gossiped about by others.

Yet, I can honestly tell you that the freedom that came from telling someone the truth was a massive step forward for me.

The enemy wants to keep us isolated and feeling alone in our pain to keep us from getting the healing we need and deserve. He wants us to believe that we are the only one who has ever experienced or felt what we have and that if others knew, they would reject us. But God has a different view. The Bible says that "the truth will set you free" (John 8:32) and there are no truer words. Obviously, I would definitely advise you to use wisdom with who you tell. There are people who thrive on gossip and do not have your best interest at heart. However, if you pray about it, the Lord will lead you to exactly the right person, at just the right time. Too many of us are silently suffering when we don't have to and are often putting off calling a friend, a counselor, or maybe even talking to a doctor. Let God shine His light on the darkest corner in your world and be courageous. He will give you His courage, strength and wisdom to tell someone your truth.

Rise To Brave!

Who do you consider to be a close Godly confidant that walks in wisdom?

_____

_____

Have you been putting off calling a counselor or a friend? Today is your day to stop carrying your burden alone or keeping the dream in your heart to yourself.

I will reach out to a friend or call a counselor by _____ (date).

"The light shines in the darkness, and the darkness has not overcome it."

John 1:8 NIV

29

MANIFESTING MY LIFE

After the divorce, I was living in a very small townhome. I had a very hard time finding a place to lease that was large enough in an area that I loved. It was rough transitioning from the life I had lived to this new reality. Although I loved the location I ended up in, the only place available at the time was a small two-bedroom townhome. The crisp air of fall had set in and with it the anticipation of Christmas. I was full of excitement and normally my home was sprinkled with decorations in every room; however this year I just did not want to have Christmas in that house, not with my four kids. It would be cramped, and drab compared to what we were used to and I truly was sad about it. Intrusive negative thoughts were fighting my desire to be grateful.

I loved the area where I was living though. It was within walking distance to a beautiful lake and the trails with trees became a place of solace and peace for me. One of the non-negotiables I had set for myself was to move my body in some form each day. With the cooler temperatures and beautiful trails, running became my new love. One day I took a different path to the lake and I came across these beautiful villa homes. I immediately thought, "Now THAT is where I want to live and have Christmas." I decided to reframe my thoughts with intentional focus on having a space that I loved again. Each day as I ran past these beautiful homes, I began thanking God out loud for providing us with one of these homes. *Thank you that I live in one of the villas. Thank you for the Christmas we will have there.* I began to picture myself and the kids celebrating our new normal life at Christmas there. I could see my Christmas wreath on the door as I passed by.

I prayed and thanked God for making a way where there seemed to be no way. Each day as I ran the same path, I would speak and say the same things. My intentions and focus were set with expectancy. But I also did MY part. I called a local listing agent and she told me there were no villas available and that all the residents living there had long term leases. She also informed me that most of the villas were leased for at least two years. It sounded bleak, but I was not deterred. I expressed my heart's desire to the Lord. I didn't try to use God as a genie, but simply asked and believed He would provide somehow, some way! Every time I ran to the lake, which was almost every day, I thanked God for the villa that He had for me. I was determined to create a new future by speaking it out loud no matter the outcome. I thanked Him for the Christmas joy we would experience there. Each time a negative thought came about Christmas with the kids in my condo, I thanked God for Christmas in the villa. I was fully convinced that God had heard my heart and would move on our behalf. I visualized what my kids looked like inside the villa and how I would decorate the home. I used all the 5 senses. What would I see and hear on Christmas morning? I thought about the smell and taste of cooking inside and I remember visualizing myself running my hand down the banister of the staircase. When there is something you desire and you ask for it, it is important that you exercise your faith by visualizing yourself having it. If you are asking God to do a miracle in your marriage, get a vision for what you two will be doing and saying when your marriage is whole and focus on that. Asking for healing and then saying things like, "My husband isn't going to change" is a divided mind and one without faith.

Weeks later, I received a call from the agent out of the blue. To her surprise, a couple living in one of the villas was being quickly transferred out of the city for work. They would have to break their lease and a villa home was immediately available. And guess what?! The move in date would be the week of Thanksgiving! I was ecstatic! I could be in this villa home for Christmas! The only problem was I had no idea if my management company would let me out of my contract at my current home; but crazy enough, my place was in high demand and easily leasable--so long story short, they let me out of the lease without paying my full contract!

We had a beautiful, joyful Christmas in the villa! All the things I prayed for and set my focus on happened. God had been so faithful (Psalm 89:8)!

We've all heard the term "manifesting". It's everywhere in the secular arena. Yes, I'm going to go there. In fact, a lot of religious people may freak out that the title of this devotional is "Manifested!" However, it is incredible to realize that God is the author of *all* things. He is the One true God who says that without faith it's impossible to please God (Hebrews 11:6) and "manifesting" is a term the secular world may use, but God's word was the original Book on believing in something that you cannot yet see. There is also scientific proof in quantum physics that is scientifically part of all God created. Most of us have seen the stories where speaking negative and harsh words to a plant literally causes them to not grow as well as the plants nurtured with loving words. Plants who are spoken to positively grow better than those who are bullied or spoken to negatively. Words become flesh and have energy! Scientifically, when we speak, the sound waves not only carry the message spoken, but also create an impact on the person receiving it. In Romans 4:17, God said to "call those things that are not as though they were". When we align with His promises and His Word and delight ourselves in Him, He will give us the desires of our heart! I believe all the Bible is true. In Mark 11:23, Jesus told us that if we would tell a mountain to be cast into the sea, and did not doubt in our heart, but believed it would be done, it would be.

I took my desire to the Lord. I asked Him boldly. I trusted by faith and I did not doubt it would happen. I thanked Him for it and envisioned it before it ever came to be. I did my part and trusted the outcome to Him. He saw fit in His goodness and kindness to give me the desire of my heart that Christmas! The key in all of this is to truly trust Him and align your mouth with what you are asking for. Talk and act in belief and faith. I didn't ask for the villa home and then speak negatively about the chances of one opening up. I aligned my words as if I already had what I asked for. So many times, we limit God with our own words and thinking. Think about the Israelites who God wanted to bring into the Promised Land, but they limited God with their complaints and lack of faith. I would not have been disappointed with God or felt He wasn't good if the outcome had been different! Would I have been a little sad? Of course, but it wouldn't have changed my relationship with Him. He is a faithful God and His provision of the villa when it seemed impossible (based on the facts) set my faith ablaze!

We know He longs to give us good gifts, so why do we make small requests and then live each day as if they are not going to happen? It may not happen when we want or even how we think it will happen, but be assured in His faithfulness, God will answer the cries of our heart if we believe without doubting. We can trust our desires with the One who has our best interest at heart! He is for you, and He is working ALL things together for your good! I would rather sound crazy and believe for huge miracles than limp through life with doubt, expecting nothing, and getting what I said. Remember, there are people in the Bible who had radical faith and believed things were done before they even asked—like the woman who believed she would be healed if she could only touch the hem of His garment. Like the man whose son was sick and believed boldly that if Jesus would just say the word without even seeing his son, he would be healed. Jesus healed his son even as the man spoke out in faith! Begin to speak and thank God for answering unreasonable prayers. Envision your future the way you want and begin to live and act as if it is true. Watch God ignite your faith as He shocks you with how good He can be!

Rise To Brave!

Surrender the desires of your heart to Him. Get into His Word and find His promises and meditate on them. Ask the Lord to make His desires your desires. He will direct and align all things and outcomes for your good.

Today, I want you to write out one desire that you have been afraid to take to the Lord. Maybe you feel like it's too silly, or too outrageous. Be bold and ask Him for an audacious request. He knows what is in your heart anyway :). Take a few minutes and write down that one thing or several. Surrender it to Him. Look up or even google scriptures on the topic. Be brave and boldly ask Him for it. Use your 5 senses. Ask the Holy Spirit to guide and direct you regarding anything you need to do to make it happen. Pray the Scriptures out loud and thank Him in advance for answering. Be a diligent guard of your words and make sure they are aligned with the posture of receiving your request. Now rest and trust Him to be the faithful God that He is! Pray right now and wait for God to do exceedingly more than you can imagine as you speak life into the glorious future He has for you. Stop putting limits on the God of the Universe!

"...And calls those things which do not exist as thought they did."

Romans 4:17b

36

LETTING GO OF REGRET

*L*iving with an addict is not for the faint of heart. It might seem like no big deal until you find yourself in a situation with one. During this season in my life, living with a spouse bound in addiction was incredibly difficult. I was exhausted, angry, and hurt. I was tired of the disruption in our family of 6 and frankly, it was one of those nights. I was angry about the financial damage and loss the addiction had brought into our lives. My husband came home very late… again. When he came in, I could tell he had been using drugs.

He began to spout off towards me. I had learned to steer clear when he was like that. What I did next does not make me proud to share, and in all transparency, I knew better than to "poke the bear" or attempt to communicate with someone who was not sober. I let my emotions get the best of me and I reacted wrongly. I looked right at him and harshly said, "I'm not putting up with it tonight and you are going to need to leave!" Well, that was all it took, and everything exploded. He started yelling and the arguing escalated. The kids' faces were alarmed as he reached to grab a hold of me. I had set him off.

I realized *"Oh my gosh he could literally hurt me in front of the kids."* My oldest shoved himself in between us and said, "Dad, you need to go." Another one of our kids screamed from upstairs, "Why are you all fighting?" The scene was traumatic for all our children.

My husband began to enlist the kids' sympathy, "Your mom starts it, you see how she talks to me!" So, my two oldest kids kept telling him, "Just go. Come on Dad, we are going with you." It felt like they were all siding with him, but what they were trying to do was diffuse the situation. So, he went out to his truck and the kids stood at his car door trying to console him. I stood at the front door and my kids were looking at me like I was awful and had provoked him. He might not have reacted the way he did if I had given no response to him and not pushed it. I knew he was incapable of being in control at that moment because he was high. But, I'm human and I reacted. I likely could have avoided a scene that left everyone hurt if I had responded instead of reacted. But the reality is, you can't be on your "A game" all the time.

This was a memory that imprisoned me with regret. Regret that if I had just kept my mouth shut, they wouldn't have had to see it and experience it. I replayed that ugly scene over and over in my mind.

I remember crying before the Lord. I felt bad about our children witnessing that situation. I apologized to the kids and owned my part, but I couldn't let go of the regret. In a moment of quiet, sitting with my mistake, it was like I almost audibly heard the Lord saying, "Kathy do you love Me?" It reminded me of the story in the Bible (John 21), where Jesus asked Peter the same question after his failure. I responded, "You know I do Lord". The Lord was firm, but full of compassion, "then you need to stop reminding yourself and let it go." I felt prompted by the Holy Spirit to write myself a letter expressing how God saw me in that moment. As the Holy Spirit led me to see the truth about how I was authentically feeling in that moment, I began to feel compassion and grace in a place of condemnation and shame. I needed to forgive myself.

The truth behind my emotional explosion was that I was afraid. I wanted my husband to show up and fix all of this. Instead, he came with blame again. I wanted our family whole. I was just so broken and as I wrote myself that letter, I realized what I genuinely wanted was actually *God's heart* as well. God wanted our family whole. God wanted a whole wife. God wanted a loving marital relationship. So, writing that letter let me see the heart behind who I was and the hurt that came out in a bad situation. The Lord reassured me that He loved me with an *everlasting* love and my failure didn't change His heart or opinion of me.

Later, that situation was part of making amends with my kids and asking them to forgive me. Asking for forgiveness can take a lot of bravery because talking about it can bring shame back up. And when we mess things up as parents, it's easy to hope our kids don't remember or that they blocked it out! But they usually do remember, so I went to them and said, "I know you remember this, and I am so sorry for my part in this. Will you please forgive me?" There was something about me asking for forgiveness and being willing to admit my part to them that was incredibly powerful. Choosing to humble myself and be brave with them will hopefully allow them to be brave in the future. If there are people you have hurt, it's time to lean into brave, make amends, and let go of your guilt. I knew at that moment that not forgiving myself denied that Jesus was enough to carry my mistakes. It would keep me from being a healed and fully present mom. I chose to forgive myself and let His everlasting love dismantle any regret. I encourage you to allow His unfathomable love to go into the holes of regret in your own heart. God will be faithful to reveal His heart to you.

Rise To Brave!

First, hear the Lord speaking to you as He did with Peter in John 21:15-17. I encourage you to read John 21 to grasp the story.

Next, fill in the blank, "_____," do you love Me?"   (Your name)

Finally, write a letter to yourself and ask the Holy Spirit to show you how you were really feeling in a situation where you feel you have failed. Let the Father's heart of love and compassion lead you to a deeper understanding of His unconditional love and forgiveness, even towards yourself.

This next exercise is important! Take a few minutes and find yourself a mirror (Yes, be brave and do it!). Then repeat these affirmations while you look into the mirror (Yes, say them out loud… your own ears need to hear it!):

- I am remarkably made. (Psalm 139:14)

- I am more than a conqueror. (Romans 8:31)

- I am strong and courageous. (Deuteronomy 31:6)

- I am free from guilt (Roman 8:1)

- God works all things for my good (Rom 8:28)

- No matter what I go through, God's glory will be revealed through my life. (Romans 8:18; Philippians 1:6)
- I have everything I need to flourish. (2 Peter 1:3)
- I overcome everything with Christ. (1 Corinthians 15:57)

"But this one thing I do, forgetting those things which are behind, and reaching forth unto those things which are before."

Phillipians 3:13

31

GOOD IS THE OUTCOME

I was in the doctor's office filling out forms for a new patient visit. There, glaring at me from the form were the words,

Marital Status: (Please check the box)

___ Single ___ Married ___ Divorced

I wanted to shout, "It's none of your dang business!" I felt the lump in my throat and the knot in my stomach. Why was this so hard? Why did such a simple question create such intense emotion?

It was the first time I had ever checked the box *Divorced*. It was like that little question was a blatant reminder of the harsh reality of being divorced. My mind tried to spiral into the pit of "what used to be" and "it's so not fair". I tried not to sink down into my chair. Yes, it was the truth. I was divorced. I, Kathy, was no longer married and living my life as normal. The truth was that nothing was normal in my life at that moment. Everything I had known for 25 years had been flipped completely upside down and inside out. I didn't want to be a divorcee.

Another truth was *it sucked*. The 'secondary losses' or triggers that come out of our painful experiences can be shockingly hard. I battled the borage of emotions until I finally landed on one thought…"It's so not fair." That statement was indeed true, it was *NOT* fair.

As I sat staring at the paper and with the truth of my thought, I knew I had to replace the negativity with a positive perspective. I allowed myself to sit in it for a few minutes. If God is good, why did my husband lose his battle with addiction? Why did the man I fell in love with hurt our family so much? Why was I left alone as a single mom of 4? I truly believed God was good, but simply couldn't reconcile the trauma events with the goodness of God. If the Lord God is a sun (life/light giving) and a shield (protection) as mentioned in the verse above, how come it feels like He is withholding "good" from me? I wasn't angry at God; I just sincerely was trying to deal with this overwhelming "It's so not fair" thought. I felt the Holy Spirit shift my perspective to His,

"Good is not about a moment, good is about the outcome. "

I remembered how God had been so faithful in the trauma. When I felt I couldn't take another breath, He carried me. When the fear overwhelmed me, His Word calmed and sustained me. When I fought to believe there was hope, He anchored me with the truth. Had this journey been unbearably painful? Absolutely. But had He ever left me? No. I honestly knew that it was only His unfathomable love that saved me and held me up in the darkness.

True, the destruction of divorce and addiction in my marriage was overwhelming, and yet now I was moving forward with hope and a future. Somehow those incredibly difficult ("no good") moments were not His designed outcome for my life. God was not withholding good from me, but working all things for my good and His glory!

The Holy Spirit had helped me shift the thought to His perspective. That was His grace that He gave (and continues to give). The pain was momentary, and God's goodness was right there in that doctor's waiting room. He even cared that it was hard for me to check the "Divorced" box. I looked back down at the medical form and checked the Divorced box and breathed a prayer. "God, You will not withhold one good thing from me. You have a plan that is good, and I believe You." Yes, the moment might not have felt good, but as I checked that box, I knew the outcome would ultimately be.

Rise To Brave!

What is one thing that triggers the onslaught of emotional thoughts for you? It may be a small thing like checking *Divorced* or it could be a huge thing. Be specific and write it below:

_____

_____

_____

_____

_____

Find a Scripture that helps you to replace the negative aspect of that thought or the circumstance that seems unfair or that you have not yet seen the promises of God fulfilled. (Feel free to use the scriptures found on my website.)

Example: 'Divorced". That came with a lot of feelings of shame and feeling alone.

It was true that I was now divorced, but that was not my only reality or the end of my story. God had a hope and a good future planned for me. I was fearfully and wonderfully made. There is no condemnation because I am in Christ Jesus. God is completing His work in me.

"For the Lord God is a sun and shield: the Lord will give grace and glory; no good thing will He withhold from those who walk uprightly."

Psalm 84:11

CONCLUSION

*F*irst, Beautiful Friend, I am so proud of you! I know it took lots of courage to walk through this book! I believe that as you took the tangible steps to build courage that the Holy Spirit met you at your point of need as He did for me. Life presents many opportunities to continue to build bravery. You don't have to go through a terrible trauma to recognize the power you have within yourself through Christ!

So many women are living in fear of being known or even being seen. I believe there is a RISING of women that want to be known and have the gumption to be SEEN! You, my dear, have taken huge steps to being a part of that unstoppable force of women.

As I typed the above words, it reminded me of a scripture that I highly recommend you remember as you continue to bravely rise!

"From the moment John stepped onto the scene until now,
the realm of heaven's kingdom is bursting forth, and
passionate people have taken hold of its power."
MATTHEW 11:12 TPT

You are one of these passionate people! By courageously choosing to take one step at a time, you are moving forward with momentum. I so believe God honors our genuine efforts and faith, even in the tiniest step of bravery! You can now be catapulted into the passion and purpose that will impact those around you.

Remember, God has a good plan and purpose for your life! (Jeremiah 29:11). HE knows you. HE sees you. HE is FOR YOU! We have IDENTITY in Him through His brave and selfless journey to the cross where He died for our sins. His victorious resurrection paid for our freedom and purpose! He is now seated at the right hand of God making intercession for us! He is truly celebrating your courage to push through your pain into the fullness of purpose for your life!

As I conclude this simple book, *31 Days to Brave*, I want to go back to the Scripture that we started with and reference the Passion Translation:

"Jesus looked at her and said, "Didn't I tell you that if you will
believe in Me, you will see God unveil His power? So, they
rolled away the heavy stone. Jesus gazed into heaven and said,
"Father thank You that You have heard My prayer, for You
listen to every word I speak. Now, so that those who stand
here with me will believe that You have sent me to the earth as
Your messenger, I will use the power You have given Me."

JOHN 11:40

Jesus looked at HER...

I love that verse. I love that He LOOKED at HER! Friends, He's looking at YOU! He's gently gazing into your eyes and reassuring you that you will see Him and His power in your trauma or difficulties! The next part of that verse is so paramount. Jesus didn't roll away the stone on Lazarus' grave. They did! They acted. They decided. They bravely believed Him! In times of gut-wrenching loss/heartache or situations that leave us almost paralyzed with grief and fear, we can know He is looking at us with love and compassion and saying to you (this is me obviously paraphrasing here) …

"Oh, I know how your soul is so grieved and it's seems impossible but didn't I say if you can just muster up a tiny bit of courage that I will show up? Look into my eyes and know I'm right here for you. You can borrow My brave and I am everything you need. Trust me. I am trustworthy. I am faithful. I'll never leave you alone in this trauma and pain. I've got you. You are going to make it. Just take a little step and then another and watch me be so big in your life! I am who I say I am and I will do what I said I will do. All things are possible, daughter. Nothing is impossible with Me!"

Don't you know the courage and bravery it must have taken Martha to stand believing in front of the grave of her dead brother? Lazarus had been dead for 4 days! But oh! When Jesus LOOKED at her and spoke… She borrowed His bravery, and her brave action revealed her belief. It's a beautiful tandem dance, our steps of bravery beget believing and then believing creates more bravery! And the dance continues and becomes more fluid and natural for the rest of our lives. It's a wonderful thing to realize that HE truly is our bravery! The finished work of the cross gives us complete access to borrow His bravery (Christ in us, the Hope of Glory)! We can walk through this life rising in our God-ordained purpose, living, and knowing that we can "take heart, be of good courage" and grow through our trials and traumas, so that we impact others along the way. And before you know it, there will be others who "borrow your bravery" as you point them to the Brave One who makes it all possible.

I believe there is a movement of women rising that will be so courageous and impact the earth like never before. Be encouraged that you are moving in that direction and don't stop! There is a call for the courageous to rise! Keep walking, keep taking the steps and following Christ's lead, keep running in search of everything He has for you! The results will be supernaturally beyond anything we could ask or think. And it all starts with baby steps because bravery is built one step at a time.

I am so proud of you. Never give up. He's fighting for you, and so am I.

Let's go RISE AS BRAVE WOMEN and CHANGE THE WORLD!

We'd love to hear from you!

Kathy Smalley is available for book signings and speaking engagements. We look forward to connecting with you! You may email us at kathy@kathysmalley.com, or message Kathy on her website at www.kathysmalley.com.

Social Media:

@kathyroseberrysmalley

@kathydsmalley